BAKING KIDS LOVE

BAKING KIDS LOVE

Sur La Table

with Cindy Mushet

PHOTOGRAPHY BY Maren Caruso

Andrews McMeel
Publishing, LLC

Kansas City • Sydney • London

For our youngest bakers, who inspire us with their enthusiasm and love for all the sweet things in life

CONTENTS

NOTES TO ADULTS

Making and sharing food with children is a gift of love that brings a family closer together and prepares children to be independent in the kitchen when they grow up. Kids love to measure and knead and mix. They want to become self-sufficient and it's our job to help them do just that. Food is a wonderful way for children to find out about themselves and about other cultures, and learning to bake reinforces a whole host of life and school skills: cooperation, self-reliance, sharing, giving, math, science, social studies, psychology, and more.

Baking with children helps to forge a deep connection. As you work together, kids open up about all kinds of things you might never hear otherwise and ask questions that are seldom voiced in quiet conversation. They also feel free to laugh and to make silly jokes. Because they are having fun in the kitchen, they are happy to spend time there, and to share what they've made.

Here are some tips to help you get the most out of your time with kids in the kitchen:

1 RELAX.

It's food, not world peace. Memories are made and lessons are learned even when disaster strikes. Remember, everything can be washed, and imperfections can be hidden. Kids are thrilled with nearly anything that comes warm from the oven. Allow that joy and wonder to fill your heart and ease your mind.

2 START SMALL AND WORK UP.

If your child has never baked before, begin with a simple one-bowl recipe, such as Mini Corn Bread Muffins (page 74) or Secret Ingredient Chocolate Chip Cookies (page 25). These are delicious and are not intimidating. Once the kids feel comfortable in the kitchen, let them choose more challenging recipes.

3 MEASURE CAREFULLY.

Most kids find baking fun. And we want it to be fun for them. But we also want good results, and that means measurements must be as precise as possible. Invest in good-quality measuring cups and spoons, and take the time to teach your kids how to measure properly (see pages 5–6).

4 CHECK YOUR OVEN'S ACCURACY REGULARLY.

Most home—and many professional—ovens are inaccurate. It's disappointing to spend a chunk of time and money on a baking project only to see it emerge ruined because the oven was off by 25 or 50 degrees. Invest in an oven thermometer to test your true oven temperature, then adjust the dial accordingly when you bake.

Here is how to test the true temperature of your oven:

* For the most reliable reading, purchase a thermometer that has a glass tube with colored liquid (usually alcohol) inside.

* Position an oven rack in the center of the oven, and set the thermometer in the center of the rack.

* Set the oven to 350°F and let it preheat for 30 minutes.

* Check the thermometer. If the oven is higher or lower than 350°F, make a note of the difference and compensate accordingly the next time you set the oven temperature.

* When you are finished testing the oven, remove the thermometer and store it safely nearby. Every month or so, retest your oven.

5 MAKE SURE YOU HAVE EVERYTHING YOU NEED FOR A RECIPE BEFORE YOU BEGIN TO BAKE.

Carefully check the list of ingredients and tools against what you have on hand. You don't want to get halfway through a recipe only to discover you don't have enough flour.

6 CHECK THE HEIGHT OF YOUR YOUNG BAKER'S WORKSPACE.

Kids should stand while working. Sitting puts the body at an angle that is not ergonomic for mixing, kneading, and decorating. Be sure there is a counter or kitchen table that is a comfortable height for them.

7 BE PREPARED FOR A BIT OF A MESS.

A little disorder is inevitable and it's also part of the fun. In the beginning, flour will drift over the side of the counter, and eggs will drip on the way to the trash can. Just remind yourself that with each baking session, the process will become neater.

8 TEACH KIDS HOW TO CLEAN.

One of the most important skills children learn is how to clean up after themselves. Keep a bowl or plastic storage container nearby for trash, so they can easily—and neatly—drop eggshells and other debris into it as they work, and then transfer the contents to a trash can later. Once the batter or dough is in the oven, put on some music and have fun while you clean.

9 TAKE YOUR KIDS GROCERY SHOPPING.

Learning how to shop for groceries is part of what kids need to know to take care of themselves. Explain to them why you choose one brand over another. Show them what to look for when picking out apples, strawberries, or other fruits. Help them learn to identify types of flour, yeast, and butter. Eventually, let them make some decisions on their own.

10 REMEMBER, ESPECIALLY FOR YOUNGER KIDS, BAKING IS MORE LIKE CRAFTING THAN MAKING SOMETHING TO EAT.

Most children like every aspect of mixing, baking, and decorating. But sometimes they are not enthusiastic about eating what they have made. Be patient. As they grow older, they will relish every bite they bake. The skills they develop along the way will pay off once their palates catch up to their kitchen abilities.

Welcome to the kitchen!

My daughter, Bella, and I love to bake. We have filled this book with recipes that we think you'll like as much as we do. I have been a pastry chef for over twenty years, and Bella has been helping me in the kitchen for eleven years. At first, she mostly just tasted things, but now she can bake all by herself. She has made every recipe in this book, and you'll find her tips throughout the pages. She gave me suggestions on what kids love to bake—things like monkey bread, pizza, chocolate cake, and lots of cookies—so the super-delicious kid-tested baked goods in this book are sure to make you happy.

When you begin baking, you are probably going to need some help from an adult. But once you feel comfortable and confident in the kitchen, and an adult approves, you will be able to make almost all of the recipes here by yourself. Turn the page and let's get started!

—Cindy

I like whole-wheat bread and I eat it sometimes, but I don't come home from school and say, "Hey Mom, I'm just dying to make some nutritious whole-wheat bread!" I've tested all of the recipes in this book, so don't worry: They are recipes kids love, not recipes adults *wish* kids would love. All of these circus-shaped boxes throughout the book contain my personal baking notes.

—Bella

LET'S BAKE!

If you measure your ingredients carefully and mix them with love, then magic will happen in the oven.

—BELLA

dressed to bake

* Tie back long hair into a ponytail.

* Wear a short-sleeved shirt, or roll up long sleeves.

* Take off any rings or dangly bracelets.

* Wear an apron and closed-toe shoes (just in case some batter or a hot cupcake drops on your foot).

> Once, I didn't want to wear an apron and ruined my favorite shirt by accidentally dragging it through melted chocolate. That was not my best day.
>
> —B

keep it clean

When you are clean and your area is clean, your food tastes better and you don't risk making yourself or others sick.

* Always wash your hands before you begin baking, and after you handle raw eggs.

* If you drop utensils on the floor, be sure to wash them before using them again.

* If you want to check the flavor of whipped cream or frosting, always use a clean spoon.

* If you want to taste raw cake batter or cookie dough, ask an adult first if it's okay (the raw eggs can make you sick).

* As you work, throw trash away—eggshells, chocolate wrappers, fruit peels—so your workspace stays clean.

* Moisten and wring out a small clean towel and use it to wipe your work surface and your hands as you work.

* Use a bench scraper to clean up flour and other dry ingredients that have gotten wet and become gummy.

* Before you begin mixing, fill up the sink halfway with warm, soapy water. As you work, drop any dirty utensils, bowls, or pans into the water. Don't drop in knives or other sharp objects. Keep those on the counter where you can see them. Once your project is in the oven, washing the dishes will take only a few minutes.

* And don't forget to sweep the floor: Flour is slippery!

> To make cleanup more fun and go faster, I put on music and dance around. See if you can finish before your favorite song ends!
>
> —B

keep it safe

* Make sure you know how to operate the electric mixer and turn on the oven. And always ask an adult for help with anything you don't understand or don't feel comfortable doing alone.

* Use oven mitts when handling hot pans. Never wear wet mitts, or the pans will burn you even faster!

* Make sure your work surface is a comfortable height. Use a sturdy step stool if the counter is too high, or use the kitchen table if it feels better to you.

* Until you are confident about your knife skills, ask for help when cutting or chopping fruit, nuts, chocolate, or other ingredients. Use a knife that fits comfortably in your hand, and always cut on a cutting board.

* If you are cutting something that rolls, like an apple, first trim a slice off one side to create a flat surface. This will keep the item stable as you finish cutting it.

ready, set, bake!

There's nothing worse than getting halfway through mixing up a batch of cupcakes only to find you are out of flour or baking powder. Always follow these steps before you begin mixing the ingredients for your recipe:

1. Read the recipe through, from start to finish. Be sure you have enough time to make it without having to rush.

2. Gather all the ingredients and tools you will need.

3. Put the oven rack in the correct position before you turn on the oven.

4. Turn on the oven and let it preheat for at least 20 minutes before you put anything into it.

5. Prepare your baking pan(s) as directed in the recipe.

6. Prepare all of your ingredients before you begin mixing. Crack the eggs into a cup or bowl. Measure the butter, sugar, and flour into separate bowls. If you have everything in front of you, mixing is easy, and you don't need to worry that you will forget something.

7. Once your project is in the oven, set a timer. It will remind you when it's time to check to see if it's done. Sometimes you can get distracted or forget, and a timer will save the day.

lining pans with parchment

1. Set your pan on a piece of parchment paper, and carefully trace around the base of the pan with a pencil (see photo).

2. Use scissors to cut along the traced line. You will end up with a piece of parchment that fits perfectly in the bottom of the pan.

greasing pans

1. Melt a little butter in the microwave, or use vegetable oil. Use a pastry brush or a paper towel to coat the inside of the pan with a thin, even layer of butter or oil. You can also use pan spray, which is quick and easy, instead of butter or oil. Just make sure it doesn't have any added flavorings, like garlic!

2. The recipes in this book don't call for dusting greased pans with flour. That's because it's not usually necessary if you are lining them with parchment. But if you want to bake a cake in one of those detailed pans that looks like a castle or a flower, or any Bundt pan, you'll need to dust the greased pan.

3. Unseasoned fine, dried bread crumbs work better than flour in the fancy pans, and they disappear during baking. Just add about ⅓ cup crumbs to the greased pan, tilt it to one side, and then twirl it to spread the crumbs into every nook and cranny and all the way to the top edge. Tap out any excess crumbs.

1

2

measuring the ingredients

Baking is a precise science. You need to measure carefully. Too much flour makes things dry, and not enough makes them flat and droopy. Too little baking powder means your cake won't rise like it should, and too much will make it fall in the center. Take your time and do it right, and you'll make fantastic breads, cakes, and cookies that taste much better than store-bought versions.

measuring dry ingredients

Dry measuring cups come in sets of graduated sizes from ¼ cup to 1 cup. They are usually metal or hard plastic and can be easily leveled at the rim.

Measuring spoons also come in graduated sets from ¼ teaspoon to 1 tablespoon, and are made of the same materials.

To measure dry ingredients:

1. Dip a dry measuring cup or measuring spoon into flour or another dry ingredient, and lift it out with the flour mounded above the rim.

2. Sweep off the excess flour with a straight edge, either the back of a table knife or the edge of an icing spatula (see photo).

3. Never press the dry ingredient into the cup or tap the cup on the work surface to pack the ingredient more tightly. Brown sugar is the exception to this rule. You need to pack it into the cup as tightly as you can by pressing down hard with your fingers. You have done it right if, when you tap it out, it is in the shape of the cup.

measuring liquid ingredients

Liquid measuring cups are made of glass or clear, hard plastic and have a pour spout. They also have lines printed on the sides that show you where to fill to for various measurements.

You can use the same measuring spoons for liquids as you do for dry ingredients. Just fill the spoon to the top edge of the spoon, and pour it into a little cup or your mixing bowl.

To measure liquid ingredients in a measuring cup:

1. Put the measuring cup on your work surface and pour the liquid into it (see photo).

2. To check if the amount is correct, lean over so you are looking at the cup at eye level. If you are not at eye level, it is difficult to tell if liquid is at the correct line.

3. If it is not at the correct line, add a little extra or pour a little out until the measurement is correct.

When I first started baking, I hated to measure. I used to make cakes by just throwing whatever I wanted into a bowl. Once I made a beautiful cake this way, but all the rest were terrible. I wouldn't even taste them. My mother always took one bite, but she could never swallow it. Be careful measuring or no one will take a bite of your cakes either!

—B

1

gathering the ingredients (mise en place)

1. As each ingredient is measured, put it into a separate bowl or container. When you think you have measured everything, double-check what you have against the recipe's ingredient list.

2. Line up all the ingredients in the order they appear in the ingredient list. This is the order in which they will be used in the recipe.

2

> If you don't want to wash lots of bowls, you can use paper muffin-cup liners, small paper cups, or pleated candy cups to hold the ingredients. As long as they are clean, place the paper cups in a resealable plastic bag and use them again and again.
>
> —B

checking for doneness in cakes and quick breads

1. Remove the cake from the oven and close the oven door. Insert a toothpick or skewer into the center of the cake.

2. Remove the toothpick and look at it carefully. If the cake is done, the toothpick will be clean or mostly clean, with just a few crumbs clinging to it (see right toothpick). If the toothpick is wet with batter (see left toothpick), return the cake to the oven and continue baking for 5 to 8 minutes, then check again.

choosing basic baking ingredients

baking soda and baking powder

Baking soda and baking powder are leaveners. They enlarge the air bubbles in your batter, which helps baked goods to rise. But baking soda and baking powder are not the same thing, and cannot be substituted for each other. Baking soda is used when recipes have acidic ingredients, and baking powder is used in recipes with more neutral ingredients. Be sure you have the right leavener before you begin a recipe.

Always check the expiration date on the box or can to make sure the contents are still good. If the date has passed, your batter may not rise properly.

buttermilk

Thick, creamy buttermilk lends both tang and tenderness to baked goods. Use fresh buttermilk if possible, though reconstituted powdered buttermilk will work, too.

chocolate

1. Unsweetened Chocolate

Unsweetened chocolate contains no sugar, so it is very bitter. The sugar in the recipe is what makes it sweet. Don't use unsweetened chocolate in recipes that call for semisweet chocolate or they will taste terrible.

2. Semisweet or Bittersweet Chocolate

Semisweet and bittersweet chocolate are two types of dark chocolate. Bittersweet has less sugar and a deeper chocolate flavor, and semisweet has a bit more sugar, so it tastes sweeter. You can use either one in the recipes in this book.

Today, the label on some bars of dark chocolate displays a percentage that tells you how much unsweetened chocolate (labeled "cacao") the bar contains. The remaining percentage is how much sugar the bar contains. For instance, a 50% bar has about 50% sugar and is nice and sweet, while a 70% bar has only 30% sugar and is much darker and more bitter in flavor. When shopping for the recipes in this book, buy bars that list 58% or less.

3. Milk Chocolate

Milk chocolate is a small amount of dark chocolate mixed with plenty of sugar and milk for a wonderful creamy flavor.

4. White Chocolate

Real white chocolate is made from cocoa butter, sugar, and milk. When shopping for it, always look at the ingredient list on the label to make sure it says "cocoa butter," which gives it a creamy color and a light, delicate flavor. Imitation white chocolate contains palm kernel oil or other fat substitutes and is snowy white.

5. Chocolate Chips

Chocolate chips come in dark, milk, and white chocolate varieties and hold their shape during baking. Keep in mind that most chocolate chips are not the same thing as real chocolate, for the natural fat of the chocolate—cocoa butter—has been removed and replaced with a substitute fat like palm kernel oil or hydrogenated vegetable oil. These substitute fats allow the chips to hold their shape in the oven. In general, do not use chips as a substitute for semisweet, milk, or white chocolate in recipes. Chips come in two sizes: regular and mini. The ingredient list will tell you which kind of chip is best for that particular recipe.

cocoa powder

Unsweetened cocoa powder for baking adds a deep chocolate flavor to desserts, but it is not the same as the mix used to make hot chocolate, so don't try to substitute that for cocoa powder. Even though unsweetened cocoa powder is very bitter, the sugar in the recipe makes it taste sweet and chocolate-y.

There are two types of unsweetened cocoa powder. Natural cocoa powder is the most common one on supermarket shelves. It is light brown in color, very acidic, and usually paired with baking soda in recipes. The other type is Dutch-process (or alkalized) cocoa powder, which is dark brown in color and usually paired with baking powder in recipes. You should not substitute these two types of cocoa powder for each other. If you are not sure which kind you have, look at the ingredient list on the package. Natural cocoa will just say "cocoa powder," while Dutch-process will say something like "cocoa powder processed with alkali."

eggs

Eggs come in many different sizes, but the recipes in this book only use large eggs. If you use another size, your recipe may not turn out like it should.

flour

Use unbleached all-purpose flour for the recipes in this book. It is better for the baked goods in this book, our bodies, and the environment.

If you use bleached flour, your recipe might be okay, but it won't turn out as well as you would like because bleached flour behaves a little differently in recipes.

milk

Use whole milk when baking. The recipes will still work if you substitute low-fat milk for whole milk, but their flavor and texture won't be quite as good.

oil

Oil makes baked goods tender and moist. Always choose clear, nearly flavorless oil for baking. Canola, corn, and safflower oil are all good choices.

sugar

Granulated white sugar is used in most baking recipes, and is called simply "sugar." Sometimes you will need light brown sugar, which is white sugar with a little molasses added for color and flavor. Dark brown sugar has more molasses and a stronger flavor. You can use dark instead of light brown sugar if you want more molasses flavor.

Powdered sugar is granulated sugar that has been ground so finely that it turns into powder. A little cornstarch is added to prevent clumping, but it's often pretty lumpy anyway. Usually you will need to sift powdered sugar, and each recipe will tell you when to sift it.

Coarse sugar, also known as sanding or large-crystal sugar, is the crunchy sugar used for decorating and comes in many colors. Turbinado sugar is also a coarse sugar, but it has a little molasses in it, which makes it light brown in color. Turbinado sugar is sometimes called "raw sugar." Do not use any of these coarse sugars in place of regular white or brown sugar in your batters and doughs.

unsalted butter

Always buy unsalted butter for baking. If you use salted butter, your cakes, pastries, and cookies can end up tasting salty.

vanilla extract

Always use pure vanilla extract. Imitation extract is made in a laboratory and does not have the natural, rich flavor of real vanilla, which is made from the fruit of an orchid flower.

yeast

Yeast are the tiny, single-celled organisms that make bread rise. These minute cells are freeze-dried and granulated into clumps that are the granules you find inside yeast packages. When you use dried yeast, you need to activate it, or wake it up, by soaking it in some warm water, usually with a little sugar.

Yeast is available in two varieties: active dry and quick rise (or instant). Both varieties are the same type of yeast cells, but the quick-rise clumps are smaller, so the yeast within the clumps is activated, or "awakened" more quickly, which can help your bread rise more quickly. Otherwise, you use them the same way when making bread.

prepping the ingredients

cracking eggs

Firmly but gently tap the middle of an egg on the rim of a bowl until you hear the egg crack. Then, holding the egg over the bowl, gently pull the shell halves apart and let the egg fall into the bowl.

separating eggs

Some recipes only use egg whites, others only egg yolks, and still others direct you to add the whites and yolks at separate points in the recipe. In any of these cases, you'll need to separate the whites from the yolks. Here's how to do it:

1. Line up 3 small clean bowls or custard cups in front of you.

2. Crack an egg (see above) over the center bowl. Begin to pull the shell halves apart, letting some of the egg white fall into the bowl, and leaving the yolk in one of the shell halves.

3. Pass the yolk back and forth between the shell halves, letting the remaining white fall into the bowl. Be careful not to poke the yolk with a sharp shell edge and break it.

4. Put the yolk in the bowl to the right. Pour the white into the bowl on the left. Repeat with the next egg.

5. If you break the yolk and it falls into the center bowl with the white, use it for scrambled eggs or for another baking recipe. Try again with another egg, but be sure to wash out the center bowl so there is no yolk left. It doesn't matter if there is a little egg white in with the yolks, but any yolk in with the whites can prevent them from whipping up into a white, fluffy froth.

softening butter

When a recipe calls for softened butter, cut cold butter into tablespoon-size pieces and arrange them around the inside of a mixing bowl. Do not let them overlap. This will help the butter to soften quickly. After 20 minutes, the butter will be soft and ready to go.

melting butter

Cut the butter into small pieces and place them in a microwaveable bowl or a small saucepan. Microwave for 30 seconds, or until just melted. If using a saucepan, heat over low flame just until melted. Use while warm and fluid. If the butter gets hard before you're ready to use it, simply melt again.

> Sometimes, a piece of shell ends up in the eggs when you are cracking or separating them. The best way to remove any little pieces is with one of the shell halves. Put it next to the piece of shell and scoop it out.
>
> —B

proofing yeast

Whenever a recipe calls for yeast, you need to "wake it up" first by dissolving it in warm liquid, usually with a little sugar. The liquid should be no hotter than 120°F, the temperature of a nice warm bath. Very hot liquid will kill the yeast, so be sure to test the temperature by touching the water with your finger. If it's too hot for you, it's too hot for the yeast.

1. Place the warm liquid in a small bowl.

2. Add the yeast and sugar and mix with a small whisk or spoon (see left cup below).

3. Set aside for 8 to 10 minutes, until it looks foamy on top (see right cup below). The yeast is now ready to use.

   If the yeast isn't foamy after 15 minutes, the liquid was too cold to wake it up, the liquid was too hot and killed it, or the yeast was too old (check the expiration date on the packet). Start over with a new packet of yeast.

sifting flour or powdered sugar

Place a medium-mesh sieve over a bowl. Add the flour and/or other dry ingredients, according to the recipe. Lift the sieve off the rim of the bowl with one hand and tap the side of the sieve firmly with the other hand. Use your fingers to push through any lumps that are left at the end.

chopping chocolate

Place the bar of chocolate on a cutting board. Using a sturdy serrated or chef's knife, cut the chocolate into small pieces by shaving down the edge of the bar, gradually moving the knife blade across the chocolate bar. A bench scraper is an easy way to pick up and transfer the chocolate to a bowl.

chopping nuts

Spread the nuts in a single layer on a cutting board. Grasping the handle of a chef's knife with one hand, and placing the fingers of your other hand on the back of the knife blade near the tip, chop the nuts, rocking the handle up and down and keeping the tip on the board. Stop when you reach the desired size.

melting chocolate

1. You will need a double boiler to melt chocolate. If you don't have one, you can substitute a medium stainless-steel or heatproof glass bowl and a medium saucepan. The bowl should rest snugly in the rim and extend about halfway into the pan.

2. Place the chopped chocolate in the top portion of the double boiler (or bowl) and set it aside on the counter.

3. Pour water about 2 inches deep into the bottom of the double boiler (or saucepan) and bring to a boil over high heat.

4. Turn off the heat and place the pan (or bowl) holding the chocolate over the steaming water. Make sure the bottom of the pan (or bowl) does not touch the water. Let sit for 2 minutes, then stir well with a clean, dry spatula. If lumps remain, let sit for another 2 minutes and stir again.

5. When the chocolate is fully melted and smooth, leave it over the warm water until you need it. That way it will remain liquid and be easier to blend into a batter. If the recipe says to cool the chocolate, remove the pan (or bowl) from over the water and set it aside until it is cool to the touch but still fluid before using.

zesting lemons or oranges

1. Wash and dry the fruit.

2. Hold the fruit in one hand and a grating rasp in your writing hand.

3. Gently pull the rasp over the surface of the fruit, turning the fruit once you have removed the zest from each area. You want to remove the pretty colored portion of the skin only, not the soft white pith underneath it, which is bitter.

juicing lemons or oranges

1. Roll the fruit back and forth on the work surface, pressing down firmly. This will help you get more juice from the fruit.

2. Cut the fruit in half crosswise. Place a half, cut side down, in a citrus squeezer. Hold the juicer over a bowl, and squeeze the handles together firmly.

3. If you have a citrus reamer, hold the fruit over a sieve placed over a cup or bowl (the sieve will catch the seeds). Hold the reamer in your writing hand and press it hard into the citrus, wiggling it back and forth until you get as much juice as possible.

hulling strawberries

1. The hull of a strawberry is the green, leafy part on the top. It is easy to remove with a strawberry huller or a 1-inch star piping tip.

2. Insert the spadelike ends of the huller or the points of the piping tip into the berry so that the greenery is in the center of it, then twist firmly and pull out the green leaves and stem.

3. If you don't have a huller or star tip, cut a little cone around the greenery with the tip of a paring knife and then pull it out with your fingers.

cleaning raspberries and blackberries

1. Pour the berries out of the container onto a baking sheet or big, flat plate.

2. Pick out any moldy berries and anything that isn't fruit—you might find stems or leaves—and put them in the trash. The berries that are left on the plate are now ready to use.

3. Don't wash them or they will fall apart.

peeling, coring, and slicing apples

1. Using a vegetable peeler, remove all of the peel from the apple (see left photo).

2. Hold the apple steady on a cutting board, and use a paring knife to cut a thin slice off the bottom of the apple so it will sit flat when upright.

3. With the apple upright, hold it steady with one hand while you cut from top to bottom about an inch from the stem, taking off ¼ of the apple. Turn the apple slightly and repeat on the remaining 3 sides. The core remaining will look like a rectangle with a stem at the top.

4. Cut the apple quarters into ¼-inch-thick slices (see right photo).

grating cheese

Cheese is much easier to grate when it is cold. Put softer cheeses in the freezer for a few minutes to firm them up before you begin. Using a box grater, hold the cheese firmly against the side (most cheese is grated on the largest holes) and then push it down the side. Watch your knuckles! Repeat until you have grated all the cheese you need. When just a small piece of cheese is left, and you are worried about grating your fingers, ask an adult to help you finish.

1   4

mixing and rolling techniques

blending dry and liquid ingredients in a bowl

This mixing technique is used for mixing muffins and some quick breads and cakes. It is the simplest and quickest method for blending ingredients.

1. Sift the dry ingredients into a large bowl. Push through any lumps with your fingers. Whisk to blend evenly.

2. Place the liquid ingredients, such as eggs and milk, in a medium bowl, and whisk until fully blended.

3. Make a well in the center of the dry ingredients, and pour the liquid ingredients into it (see photo). Whisk gently at first, and then, as the dry and liquid ingredients begin to blend, whisk faster, stopping when you have a smooth batter and no dry patches are visible. A few small lumps are okay.

creaming butter and sugar

This mixing method is used for cakes and cookies. It blends together butter and sugar, creating millions of little air bubbles in the butter. When these bubbles get hot in the oven, they expand, causing your baked goods to rise.

1. Put the softened butter and the sugar in a bowl.

2. Start the mixer on low, so that your ingredients don't fly out of the bowl, and beat the butter and sugar until blended. Then turn the mixer speed to medium.

3. For most cookie recipes, beat for only 2 minutes, or until smooth and just slightly lightened in color (see top of photo).

4. For most cake recipes, you will need to beat longer, usually 5 to 7 minutes, until the batter is almost white (see bottom of photo).

3

4

cutting in the butter

This method is used for biscuit dough, crumble topping, and pie dough.

1. Cut the cold butter into small cubes and refrigerate for 10 minutes.

2. Put all of your dry ingredients into a mixing bowl and whisk until well blended. Don't put in any chocolate chips or raisins or other chunky items yet. Those are mixed in at the very end.

3. Scatter the cold butter cubes over the dry ingredients (see top of photo).

4. Using a pastry blender or 2 table knives, cut the butter with quick chopping motions into smaller and smaller pieces. Every once in a while, use a table knife or small metal spatula to scrape off any butter that gets stuck in the wires of the pastry blender.

5. Continue until the largest pieces of butter are the size of green peas, or even smaller when making pie dough (see bottom of photo). Some pieces of butter will be smaller, and that's fine. Then, continue with the recipe as directed.

3

5

whipping egg whites

Make sure your bowl and beaters are very clean before you begin. Any grease or fat will prevent egg whites from whipping into an airy mixture.

1. Carefully separate the eggs (see page 10) and transfer the whites to a clean mixing bowl.

2. Start the mixer on medium-low and beat the whites for 1 minute to break them up. They will start to look bubbly and frothy.

3. Turn the mixer speed to medium-high and continue beating until soft peaks form. The whites should look like whipped cream. To check for soft peaks, turn off the mixer, lift the beaters straight out, and then turn them upside down. The slope leading to the tip should be soft and barely holding its shape.

4. Turn the mixer back on to medium-high speed and gradually sprinkle in the sugar. It should look like a gentle rain falling into the whites. Once you've added all of the sugar, beat for 15 seconds longer, then turn off the mixer. Turn the beaters upward again to check for firm peaks. The whites should stand on top of the beaters in nearly vertical, firm peaks, even if the tip falls over at the end. If the slope is still soft and bent over, beat for another 30 seconds and check again.

whipping cream

Put the heavy whipping cream and sugar into a bowl. You can whip by hand with a whisk or use a mixer. If you use a handheld mixer, turn it to low speed and beat for 1 minute, then turn the speed to medium and continue to beat until the cream is thick and looks like mayonnaise. Turn off the mixer and lift the beaters out of the bowl. If the cream holds a soft peak when the beaters are lifted, it is ready. If it doesn't, beat a little longer. Be careful you don't overbeat. If you beat too long, the cream will look grainy, or even like cottage cheese. If this happens, add another 3 to 4 tablespoons cream and stir in gently with a silicone spatula (no more whipping!). This should smooth out the whipped cream. If not, stir in a little more cream.

kneading

You must knead bread dough so it will rise and hold its shape.

1. Sprinkle a little flour on your work surface (don't put too much, because you can always add more later). Dip your hands in flour. Set the mound of dough in front of you on the work surface. Using the heel of both hands, firmly push the top of the mound away from you (see left photo).

2. Fold the far side of the dough toward you (see right photo), then rotate the mound of dough a quarter turn and push again.

3. Keep kneading until you get a smooth, springy dough. It usually takes 8 to 10 minutes.

4. To know if you have kneaded enough, press your hand into the dough and remove it quickly. Your handprint should bounce back and disappear quickly. If it doesn't, keep kneading.

1   2

6

rolling out dough

This method is used for pies, tarts, biscuits, cookies, and cinnamon rolls.

1. Sprinkle 3 to 4 tablespoons flour all over your work surface.

2. Put the dough directly in front of you and sprinkle a little more flour over the top. Start with the dough in the shape you want it to be eventually: If you are rolling out a circle, have the dough shaped in a circle. If you want to end up with a rectangle, begin with a rectangle.

3. Starting from the edge closest to you, roll gently but firmly to the edge opposite you. Lift the

rolling pin just as you get to the far edge. If you roll off the edge of the dough onto the work surface, you'll cause the edge to stick to the work surface.

4. Now, if you are rolling out a circle, pretend the circle of dough is a clock face, with 12 o'clock at the top. Turn the dough 2 hours clockwise, to 2 o'clock, and then roll up and back again twice. Rotate the dough 2 more hours clockwise and roll up and back again twice. When you turn the dough, it should move easily. If it doesn't, gently lift the area of the dough that is stuck, loosen it with a small metal spatula,

and sprinkle a little more flour under it. Repeat until the dough is the size, shape, and thinness described in the recipe.

5. If you want to roll out a rectangle, use the same technique, but give the dough a quarter turn each time.

6. When you have finished rolling, brush any extra flour from the top (see photo). Scrape any excess flour from the work surface around the dough and put it in the trash. Gently fold the dough over and brush all the flour from the bottom of the dough.

in and out of the oven

* Each recipe will tell you where the oven rack should be. Before you turn on the oven, position the rack as directed.

* Turn on the oven at least 20 minutes before you put anything into it to bake. If you don't preheat for at least that long, it won't be hot enough to bake your batter or dough properly.

* Always wear dry oven mitts when you put something into or take something out of the oven. They will protect your hands and forearms from possible burns.

* If you're nervous about transferring things in and out of a hot oven or carrying hot pans, ask an adult for help.

Baking is a lot like art projects; it's easier when you have the right tools. It can get messy, but it's a lot easier to clean than paint or glue! And there's always something delicious to eat at the end.

—B

tools and equipment

You can't play a game without all the pieces, and the same is true in baking. It's hard to make great stuff when you are missing key tools. Each recipe in the book tells you exactly what tools and equipment you'll need. This list puts all the "pieces" together in one place. If you are just starting to bake, you'll need many of the items in the first and second columns (you probably already have many of them in your kitchen). If you are a regular baker, check out the third column for some of the more specialized items called for in the recipes.

the basics

tools

Bench scraper

Bowls: nesting set of 4 or 5
stainless-steel bowls

2 cooling racks

Cutting board

Electric mixer: handheld

Knives: chef's, paring, serrated

Measuring cups and spoons:
nesting set of dry measuring cups
and measuring spoons, and a 1-cup
liquid measuring cup

Offset spatula: small

Oven mitts

Parchment paper

Pastry blender

Pastry brush: larger one for brushing
flour off of dough (never wash after
use), and smaller one for applying
egg wash to a bread or buttering a
pan (wash after every use)

Rolling pin

Ruler

Medium-mesh sieve

Silicone spatula

Timer

Vegetable peeler

Whisk: 1 large and 1 small

Wooden spoon

pans

Baking sheets:
2, with ½-inch sides

9-inch round cake pans:
2, with 1½-inch sides

8-inch square cake pan
with 1½-inch sides

9 by 5-inch loaf pan

12-cup standard muffin pan

9-inch pie dish

Saucepans:
1 small and 1 medium

the next step

12 by 9-inch baking dish or pan

9-inch springform pan with
2- to 3-inch sides

Box grater

10-inch Bundt pan

10-inch round cake pan, with
1½-inch sides

Digital instant-read thermometer

Double boiler

Ice-cream scoops: for shaping
cookie dough and portioning muffin
batter

Handheld citrus squeezer or reamer

Mini muffin pan, with 24 cups

Offset spatula: large

Pizza wheel

12-inch pastry bag and ⅜-inch
plain and star piping tips

6-cup popover pan

Rasp grater

14 by 4-inch tart pan with
removable bottom

COOKIES

My favorite part about making
cookies is eating them warm.

—BELLA

These are chewy yet crispy, sweet yet salty, oatmeal-like yet packed with chocolate chips. When I bite into one, I'm in cookie heaven, surrounded by more cookies that have little halos and wings, sitting on clouds.

—B

SECRET INGREDIENT CHOCOLATE CHIP COOKIES

ingredients

1 cup (2 sticks) unsalted butter, softened (see page 10)

4 large eggs, at room temperature

1 tablespoon pure vanilla extract

1 cup canola or corn oil

4 cups unbleached all-purpose flour

2 cups sugar

2 cups tightly packed light brown sugar

2¼ cups old-fashioned rolled oats or quick oats (not instant)

2 teaspoons salt

2 teaspoons baking soda

2½ cups Kellogg's Corn Flakes (for best results, stick to this brand)

1 (12-ounce) bag miniature semisweet chocolate chips

tools

Measuring cups and spoons

2 baking sheets

Parchment paper

2 large bowls

Wooden spoon

Whisk

1-gallon-size resealable plastic bag

Spring-loaded ice-cream scoop (optional): 3 tablespoon (for big cookies) or 1 tablespoon (for regular-size cookies)

Oven mitts

2 cooling racks

before you begin

✳ Position 1 oven rack in the top ⅓ of the oven and 1 oven rack in the bottom ⅓ of the oven, and preheat the oven to 350°F. Line the baking sheets with the parchment paper (see page 4).

mix the dough

✳ Put the butter, eggs, and vanilla in 1 of the large bowls and stir with the wooden spoon until blended. Add the oil and beat well until combined. It will look like a mess, but that's okay.

✳ Put the flour, sugar, brown sugar, oats, salt, and baking soda in the other large bowl and whisk until blended. Add the dry ingredients to the butter mixture and stir well with the spoon. You can even use your hands to squish all the ingredients together. Sometimes your hands are the best tools.

✳ Put the corn flakes into the resealable plastic bag, squeeze out the air, and seal the top. Squeeze the bag until the flakes are broken into tiny pieces (do not use a food processor; it grinds the flakes too small). Add the crushed flakes and the chocolate chips to the dough and stir until evenly blended.

3

shape the cookies

* Use the large (3 tablespoon) or small (1 tablespoon) ice-cream scoop to shape the dough into cookies. You can also shape the dough by measuring out level tablespoons—3 for each big cookie, 1 for each smaller cookie—and then rolling the dough between your palms into balls.

* If you are making large cookies, bake only 6 at a time on each baking sheet, spacing the balls about 4 inches apart. These cookies spread when they bake, and if you put too many on the pan, they will run together. If you are making the smaller cookies, you can fit 12 cookies on each pan. Space them about 2 inches apart into 4 rows with 3 cookies in each row. Press down on each ball with your palm to flatten slightly.

4

bake the cookies

* Place 1 baking sheet on each oven rack. Bake the large cookies for 7 minutes or the smaller cookies for 6 minutes. Using the oven mitts, switch the pans between the oven racks. Bake until light golden brown, another 7 to 8 minutes for the large cookies, or 6 to 7 minutes for the smaller cookies.

* Using the oven mitts, transfer the pans to the cooling racks and let the cookies cool completely (if you can wait that long). You may need to reuse the pans to finish baking all the cookies. Let the pans cool before you put more dough on them for baking. Store the cookies in an airtight container or resealable plastic bag for up to 1 week.

thinking ahead

You can bake some of the cookies today, and freeze the rest of the dough balls for another day. Put the balls close together on a pan and freeze for 30 minutes, or until hard. Transfer the frozen balls to a resealable plastic freezer bag, and freeze for up to 3 months. To bake, take out as many cookies as you need, and space them on parchment-lined baking sheets as directed. Let them thaw for 15 minutes, then press down on them to flatten slightly, and bake as directed.

CHEWY OATMEAL COOKIES

ingredients

½ cup (1 stick) unsalted butter, softened (see page 10)

½ cup tightly packed light brown sugar

½ cup sugar

1 large egg, at room temperature

1½ teaspoons pure vanilla extract

1 cup unbleached all-purpose flour

½ teaspoon baking soda

¼ teaspoon salt

¼ teaspoon ground cinnamon

1½ cups old-fashioned rolled oats

¾ cup dried cranberries

tools

Measuring cups and spoons

2 baking sheets

Parchment paper

1 large and 1 medium bowl

Electric mixer

Silicone spatula

Whisk

Spring-loaded ice-cream scoop (optional): 1 tablespoon

Oven mitts

2 cooling racks

1 before you begin

✷ Position 1 oven rack in the top ⅓ of the oven and 1 oven rack in the bottom ⅓ of the oven, and preheat the oven to 350°F. Line the baking sheets with the parchment paper (see page 4).

Bella's tip: Oatmeal is good for you, and so are dried cranberries, so your mom might just let you eat these cookies for breakfast!

2 mix the dough

✷ Put the butter and both sugars in the large bowl. Using the mixer, beat on low speed for 1 minute. Turn up the speed to medium and beat for another minute. The mixture should be blended and smooth. Using the spatula, scrape down the sides of the bowl. Add the egg and vanilla and beat on medium-low speed until well blended. Turn off the mixer. Scrape down the sides of the bowl.

✷ Put the flour, baking soda, salt, and cinnamon in the medium bowl and whisk until blended. Add the dry ingredients to the butter mixture and beat on low speed just until only a few patches of flour remain. Add the oats and cranberries and continue to beat on low speed until no patches of flour are visible and the ingredients are evenly blended. Scrape down the bowl and make sure there are no clumps of flour hiding in the bottom of the bowl.

shape the cookies

* Use the ice-cream scoop to shape the dough into cookies. You can also shape the dough by measuring out 1 level tablespoon for each cookie, and then rolling the dough between your palms into a ball. Space the balls about 1½ inches apart on the prepared baking sheets.

bake the cookies

* Place 1 baking sheet on each oven rack. Bake for 7 minutes, then, using the oven mitts, switch the pans between the oven racks. Bake for another 6 to 7 minutes, until the cookies are golden brown around the edges.

* Using the oven mitts, transfer the pans to the cooling racks and let the cookies cool completely. You may need to reuse the pans to finish baking all the cookies. Let the pans cool before you put more dough on them for baking. Store in an airtight container or a resealable plastic bag for up to 1 week.

playing around

You can substitute raisins, currants, dried cherries, chopped dried apricots—whatever you like—for the dried cranberries. You can even leave the dried fruit out! If you want, you can add ⅓ cup of chopped nuts or chocolate chips for extra flavor.

MERINGUE CRISPIES

makes about
60
fun-shaped
cookies

ingredients

3 large egg whites (see page 10)

¾ cup sugar

Colored sugar or candy-coated almonds, for decorating

tools

Measuring cups and spoons

2 baking sheets

Parchment paper

Large bowl

Electric mixer

14-inch pastry bag and a ⅜-inch round plain tip

① before you begin

✳ Position 1 oven rack in the top ⅓ of the oven and 1 oven rack in the bottom ⅓ of the oven, and preheat the oven to 225°F. Line the baking sheets with the parchment paper (see page 4).

② make the meringue

✳ Be sure your bowl and beaters are very clean and there is not a speck of yolk in the egg whites. Any dirt or grease will prevent the whites from whipping. Put the egg whites in the large bowl. Using the mixer, beat on medium speed until they look like whipped cream and form soft peaks (see page 17). To check, turn off the mixer, lift the beaters straight out, and then turn them upside down. The slope leading to the tip should be soft and barely holding its shape.

✳ With the mixer on medium speed, add the sugar, about ¼ cup at a time, shaking it gently over the bowl and letting it blend in slowly. Once all the sugar has been added, turn the mixer to high speed and continue to beat for 1 to 2 minutes, until the mixture is very fluffy and shiny and forms firm peaks. This is a meringue. Turn off the mixer and check the peaks again. At this point, the slope should be nearly vertical.

3

pipe the cookies

✳ Put the tip into the pastry bag. Spoon the meringue into the bag until it is half full. Grasp the bag just above the mound of meringue and twist it 3 times (this prevents the mixture from coming out the wrong end of the bag).

✳ Squeeze from the twisted part of the bag, while guiding the bag with a couple of fingers near the tip. Pipe the meringue onto the prepared baking sheets into any shape you like: letters of the alphabet, rounds, or zigzags, for example. Keep the tip of the bag about 1 inch from the surface of the pan, and let the meringue fall out of the bag onto the pan in a thick rope (see photos).

✳ Once the bag is empty, untwist, open the top, and fill with the remaining meringue. Retwist and continue piping until you have used all the meringue. If you like, sprinkle the cookies with colored sugar.

bake the cookies

✳ Place 1 baking sheet on each oven rack. Bake for 1 hour. Turn off the oven and leave the pans inside overnight to finish drying the meringues. Tape a note to the oven door reminding your family not to turn on the oven!

✳ In the morning, remove the cookies from the oven and store them in an airtight container at room temperature. They will keep for up to 8 weeks, as long as they are kept dry.

playing around

rattling meringue bones and fingers

FOR BONES: Pipe the meringue into a stretched version of dog-bone treats.

FOR FINGERS: Pipe a straight line with a knobby center for the knuckle and a tapered end for the fingernail. Just before baking, set a colored candy almond or an almond slice into the meringue at the tapered end for a fingernail. Once the "fingers" have dried, dip the end opposite the fingernail into melted red coating chocolate for blood. Pipe a fancy ring on the finger with melted colored coating chocolate, and embellish it with "jewels" of colored sugars, dragées, or candy pearls.

When you bite into these cookies they are very crunchy, and then they melt in your mouth like cotton candy. They are also delicious dipped into melted chocolate. Make these on a dry day, or they will end up chewy instead of crispy.

—B

PERFECT PEANUT BUTTER COOKIES

ingredients

cookies

½ cup (1 stick) unsalted butter, softened (see page 10)

½ cup tightly packed light brown sugar

½ cup sugar

1 large egg, at room temperature

1 teaspoon pure vanilla extract

¾ cup creamy peanut butter (or chunky, if you like), at room temperature

1¾ cups unbleached all-purpose flour

½ teaspoon baking soda

¼ teaspoon salt

to finish

⅓ cup sugar

tools

Measuring cups and spoons

2 baking sheets

Parchment paper

1 large, 1 medium, and 1 small bowl

Electric mixer

Silicone spatula

Whisk

Spring-loaded ice-cream scoop (optional): 1 tablespoon

Table fork

Oven mitts

2 cooling racks

before you begin

* Position 1 oven rack in the top ⅓ of the oven and 1 oven rack in the bottom ⅓ of the oven, and pre-heat the oven to 350°F. Line the baking sheets with the parchment paper (see page 4).

mix the dough

* Put the butter and both sugars in the large bowl. Using the mixer, beat on low speed for 1 minute. Turn up the speed to medium and beat for another minute. The mixture should be blended and smooth. Turn off the mixer. Using the spatula, scrape down the sides of the bowl. Add the egg and vanilla and beat on low speed until well blended. Add the peanut butter and beat until well mixed. Turn off the mixer. Scrape down the sides of the bowl.

* Put the flour, baking soda, and salt in the medium bowl and whisk until blended. Add the dry ingredients to the butter mixture and beat on low speed just until the dough is smooth and no patches of flour are visible. Turn off the mixer. Scrape down the bowl one last time, and make sure no clumps of flour are hiding in the bottom.

3
shape the cookies

✳ Use the ice-cream scoop to shape the dough into cookies. You can also shape the dough by measuring out 1 level tablespoon for each cookie, and then rolling the dough between your palms into a ball. Space the balls about 2 inches apart on the prepared baking sheets.

✳ To finish the cookies, put the sugar in the small bowl. Dip the fork into the sugar and press down firmly on top of each ball once in each direction, to form a crisscross pattern (see photo). Be sure to dip the fork into the sugar before you press down on each ball, to prevent the fork from sticking to the dough.

4
bake the cookies

✳ Place 1 baking sheet on each oven rack. Bake for 5 minutes, then, using the oven mitts, switch the pans between the oven racks. Bake for another 6 to 7 minutes, until the cookies are golden brown around the edges.

✳ Using the oven mitts, transfer the pans to the cooling racks and let the cookies cool completely. You may need to reuse the pans to finish baking all the cookies. Let the pans cool before you put more dough on them for baking. Store the cookies in an airtight container or a resealable plastic bag for 5 days.

Sometimes, before baking, instead of pressing the cookies with a fork, I make a well in the center with my thumb and fill them with my favorite jelly.

—B

SMILE COOKIES

ingredients

cookies

1 cup (2 sticks) unsalted butter, softened (see page 10)

½ cup powdered sugar

1½ tablespoons pure vanilla extract

2¼ cups unbleached all-purpose flour

to finish

1½ cups powdered sugar

tools

Measuring cups and spoons

2 baking sheets

Parchment paper

Large bowl

Electric mixer

Silicone spatula

Oven mitts

2 cooling racks

Fine-mesh sieve

before you begin

* Position 1 oven rack in the top ⅓ of the oven and 1 oven rack in the bottom ⅓ of the oven, and preheat the oven to 350°F. Line the baking sheets with the parchment paper (see page 4).

mix the dough

* Put the butter and sugar in the bowl. Using the mixer, beat for about 1 minute on low speed. Turn up the speed to medium and beat for 5 to 6 minutes, until very light, almost white, in color (see page 15). Turn off the mixer. Using the spatula, scrape down the sides of the bowl. Add the vanilla and mix on medium for another 30 seconds. Turn off the mixer. Scrape down the bowl.

* Add the flour and mix on low speed just until the flour is completely blended. Scrape down the bowl one last time, and make sure no clumps of flour are hiding in the bottom.

shape the cookies

* To shape each cookie, break off a piece of dough that measures 1 level tablespoon. Roll the pieces on your work surface back and forth with your fingertips, shaping them into logs that are 3 inches long. As you do this, put a little extra pressure at the ends of the logs, so they are pointed. Place on a prepared baking sheet, shaping each log into a smile. Repeat to make more smiles, spacing them 1 inch apart on the baking sheets.

bake the cookies

* Place 1 baking sheet on each oven rack. Bake for 7 minutes, then, using the oven mitts, switch the pans between the oven racks. Bake for another 8 to 9 minutes, until the cookies are a light sand color and firm to the touch. They should be golden brown across the bottom and around the edges, but still fairly light on top. Using the oven mitts, transfer the pans to the cooling racks and let the cookies cool on the pans for 10 minutes.

finish the cookies

✳ Wash and dry the large bowl. Sift the powdered sugar into the bowl (see page 11). While the cookies are still warm, roll each one in the sugar until it is completely coated, then return it to the pan to finish cooling. When the cookies are cool, roll them in the powdered sugar again so they are thickly coated and silky white. Store in an airtight container at room temperature for up to 1 week. If the powdered sugar becomes moist or soaks into the cookies, roll them again in powdered sugar just before serving.

"These squares are soft and chewy and filled with lots of caramel-y flavors. The crunchy little toffee bits melt into pools of sweetness in the dough.

—B

MILK CHOCOLATE TOFFEE BARS

makes

36

chewy squares

before you begin

* Position an oven rack in the center of the oven, and preheat the oven to 350°F. Turn the pan upside down and mold a piece of aluminum foil to the outside. You should have about an inch of overhang around the edges. Slide the foil off the pan bottom, and turn the pan right side up. Slip the foil inside the pan. Fold down any foil that extends past the top edges over the outsides. Lightly butter the foil, or use pan spray.

mix the dough

* Put the butter and sugar in the large bowl. Using the mixer, beat on low speed for 1 minute. Turn up the speed to medium and beat for another minute. The mixture should be blended and smooth. Turn off the mixer. Using the spatula, scrape down the sides of the bowl. Add the egg and vanilla and beat on medium-low speed until well blended. Turn off the mixer. Scrape down the sides of the bowl.

* Put the flour, baking powder, and salt in the medium bowl and whisk until blended. Add the dry ingredients to the butter mixture and beat on low speed just until no patches of flour are visible. Add the chocolate chips and toffee bits and continue to beat on low until they are evenly blended in the mixture.

fill the pan and bake

* Using the spatula, scrape the dough into the prepared pan, and smooth the top in an even layer. Bake for 35 to 40 minutes, until the top is golden brown. Using the oven mitts, transfer the pan to a cooling rack and let cool completely.

4

unmold and cut

* To remove the big bar from the pan, grasp the foil at the top in 2 places opposite each other and gently pull upward. Set the big bar on a cutting board, and gently peel off the foil. Using the chef's knife, and starting at one side, cut the square into 6 equal strips. Then cut 6 equal strips in the opposite direction. You will have 36 bars. Of course, you can cut the cookies larger or smaller, if you like. Store in an airtight container or a resealable plastic bag for up to 4 days.

ingredients

½ cup (1 stick) unsalted butter, softened (see page 10)

1 cup tightly packed light brown sugar

1 large egg, at room temperature

2 teaspoons pure vanilla extract

1¼ cups unbleached all-purpose flour

1 teaspoon baking powder

¼ teaspoon salt

½ cup milk chocolate chips

½ cup toffee baking bits

tools

Measuring cups and spoons

8-inch square baking pan

Aluminum foil

1 large and 1 medium bowl

Electric mixer

Silicone spatula

Whisk

Oven mitts

Cooling rack

Cutting board

Chef's knife

Ruler

ingredients

crust

1½ cups fine graham cracker crumbs

1 tablespoon sugar

6 tablespoons (¾ stick) unsalted butter, melted (see page 10)

brownie filling

6 ounces semisweet chocolate

½ cup (1 stick) unsalted butter, cut into pieces

¾ cup sugar

2 large eggs, at room temperature

2 teaspoons pure vanilla extract

½ cup unbleached all-purpose flour

⅛ teaspoon salt

½ cup milk chocolate chips

1¼ cups mini marshmallows

tools

Measuring cups and spoons

9-inch square baking pan

Aluminum foil

1 medium and 1 large bowl

Medium saucepan

Silicone spatula

Oven mitts

Cooling rack

Cutting board

Serrated knife

Whisk

Chef's knife

Ruler

BROWNIE S'MORES BARS

before you begin

✱ Position an oven rack in the center of the oven, and preheat the oven to 350°F. Turn the pan upside down and mold a piece of aluminum foil to the outside. You should have about an inch of overhang around the edges. Slide the foil off the pan bottom, and turn the pan right side up. Slip the foil inside the pan. Fold down any foil that extends past the top edges over the outsides. Lightly butter the foil, or use pan spray.

② make and bake the crust

✱ Place the graham cracker crumbs and sugar in the medium bowl. Pour the butter over the cookie crumbs and stir with the silicone spatula until the mixture is evenly moistened. Smash any lumps that form.

✱ Scrape the mixture into the prepared pan and use your clean fingers to press it into an even layer over the bottom of the pan.

✱ Bake for 10 minutes. Using the oven mitts, transfer the pan to the cooling rack and let cool for 15 minutes. Leave the oven on.

make the brownie filling

✱ Put the chocolate on the cutting board. Using the serrated knife, chop the chocolate into small pieces (see page 11). Put the butter in the medium saucepan, place over low heat, and heat until it melts. Turn off the heat, and move the pan to a heatproof surface. Add the chocolate to the pan, let it sit for 2 minutes, then whisk until blended. The chocolate should be very smooth. If it is still lumpy, let it sit for another minute or two, then whisk again. Scrape the chocolate mixture into the large bowl.

✱ Whisk the sugar into the chocolate mixture until fully blended. Whisk in the eggs, one at a time, blending well after each egg is added. Whisk in the vanilla. Finally, whisk in the flour and salt. Whisk slowly at first, then faster, until the batter is smooth and shiny. It will be thick. Stir in the chocolate chips.

fill the pan and bake

❋ Using the spatula, scrape the batter into the crust and smooth the top. Bake for 25 minutes. Using the oven mitts, remove the pan from the oven, set it on a heat-proof surface, and close the oven door. Carefully sprinkle the mini marshmallows evenly over the top. With your hand covered by an oven mitt, gently press on the marshmallows just once so they stick to the brownie filling. You may want to ask an adult to help you with this step (see photo).

❋ Return the pan to the oven and continue to bake for another 15 minutes, or until the brownie mixture feels firm when lightly pressed, a toothpick inserted into the center comes out with a few moist crumbs on it, and the marshmallows are golden brown. Using the oven mitts, transfer to the cooling rack and let cool completely.

unmold and cut

❋ To remove the big brownie from the pan, grasp the foil at the top in 2 places opposite each other and gently pull upward. Set the big brownie on a cutting board, and then gently peel back the foil.

❋ Spray the chef's knife with a little pan spray so the sticky brownies won't cling to it when you cut them. Keep a warm, damp towel handy so you can wipe and respray the knife when it gets too messy (you may want to ask an adult to help you with this step). Starting at one side, cut the square into 6 equal strips. Then, cut 6 equal strips in the opposite direction. You will have 36 brownies. Of course, you can cut the brownies larger or smaller, if you like. Lift the brownies off the foil bottom. Store in an airtight container or a resealable plastic bag for up to 5 days.

Bella's tip: **Don't completely cover the surface of the brownies with marshmallows, or they will be impossible to cut through after baking. If you want extra marshmallows, add them to the top after you cut the bars.**

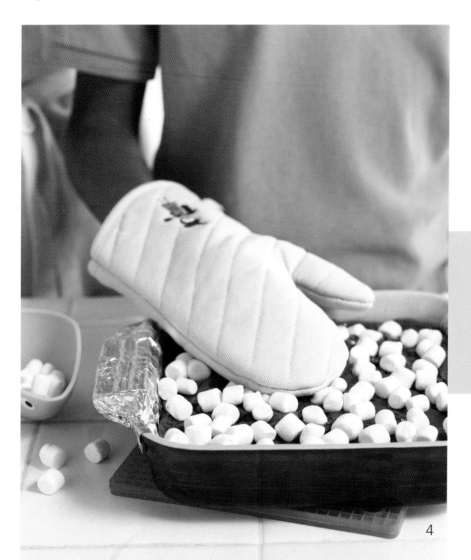

4

These cookies are a tasty way to express your creativity. Cut them into fun or unusual shapes, then decorate them with colored icings, decorating sugars, or sprinkles in your own special style. Have a cookie decorating party so your friends can join in the fun.

—B

BE CREATIVE SUGAR COOKIES

before you begin

* Position 1 oven rack in the top ⅓ of the oven and 1 oven rack in the bottom ⅓ of the oven, and preheat the oven to 350°F. Line the baking sheets with the parchment paper (see page 4).

mix the dough

* Put the butter and sugar in 1 of the large bowls. Using the mixer, beat on low speed for 1 minute. Turn up the speed to medium and beat for another minute. The mixture should be blended and smooth. Turn off the mixer. Using the silicone spatula, scrape down the sides of the bowl. Add the egg and vanilla and beat on medium-low speed until well blended. Turn off the mixer. Scrape down the sides of the bowl.

* Put the flour and salt into 1 of the medium bowls and whisk until blended. Add the dry ingredients to the butter mixture and beat on low speed just until the ingredients are blended and no patches of flour are visible. The mixture will have the texture of gravel and pebbles. Scrape down the bowl one last time, and make sure no clumps of flour are hiding in the bottom. Dump the clumps of dough onto your work surface, and squeeze them together until they form a cohesive dough. Flatten the dough into a 9-inch circle, wrap in plastic or parchment, and chill for 30 minutes before continuing.

ingredients

cookies

1 cup (2 sticks) unsalted butter, softened (see page 10)

¾ cup sugar

1 large egg, at room temperature

2 teaspoons pure vanilla extract

2¼ cups unbleached all-purpose flour

¼ teaspoon salt

icing

3 cups powdered sugar

¼ cup meringue powder

½ cup water

Food coloring, in various colors

to decorate

Sprinkles, sugar pearls, large crystal sugar, dragées, and/or candies

tools

Measuring cups and spoons

2 baking sheets

Parchment paper

2 large, 2 medium, and 2 to 4 small bowls

Electric mixer

Silicone spatula

Whisk

Plastic wrap

Rolling pin

3-inch cookie cutters

Oven mitts

Cooling rack

Sieve

1 or more small offset spatulas or small spoons

Small disposable piping bags or other piping tools (optional)

roll the dough

* Place a large sheet of parchment paper on your work surface, about the size of a baking sheet. Have a second parchment sheet the same size ready. Remove the dough from the refrigerator and place it in the center of the first parchment sheet. Top with the second parchment sheet, and flatten the dough slightly. Using the rolling pin, and starting from the edge closest to you, roll gently but firmly to the edge opposite you and then back again twice. Be careful not to roll the pin off the edge of the dough, or the dough will stick to the paper. Turn the dough, between the parchment paper, a quarter turn and roll up and back again twice. Repeat rolling up and back and turning until the dough is ¼ inch thick.

* If the paper creases into the dough, gently peel back the paper, straighten it out, and smooth it back on top of the dough. You'll need to do this several times during the rolling process. If the dough gets too soft and squishy while you are rolling, transfer it to a baking sheet (still between the parchment paper) and refrigerate for 10 to 15 minutes, until cool but flexible.

cut out the shapes

* Peel off the top sheet of parchment. If the dough is soft and sticky, refrigerate for 15 minutes. Using the cookie cutters, press down firmly to cut out shapes (see photos). Cut them as close together as possible. Using a small offset spatula, lift the shapes off the parchment paper and transfer to the prepared pans, spacing them about 1 inch apart. Press all the dough scraps together, roll the dough out, and cut out more shapes.

4

bake the cookies

* Place 1 baking sheet on each oven rack. Bake for 8 minutes, then, using the oven mitts, switch the pans between the oven racks. Bake for another 5 to 9 minutes, until the cookies are golden brown around the edges and lightly golden in the center. Using the oven mitts, transfer the pans to the cooling racks and let the cookies cool completely before decorating. You may need to reuse the pans to finish baking all the cookies. Let the pans cool before you put more dough on them for baking.

make the icing

* Sift the powdered sugar into the other medium bowl (see page 11). Put the meringue powder and water in the other large bowl. Make sure the bowl and your mixer beaters are very clean so the icing will whip up nicely. Beat the meringue on medium speed for about 1 minute, then turn the mixer to high and continue to whip until the mixture looks like whipped cream and has formed soft peaks (see page 17).

* With the mixer on medium speed, add the sifted sugar, about ¼ cup at a time, shaking it gently over the bowl and letting it blend in slowly. Once all the sugar has been added, turn the mixer to high speed and continue to beat for 1 to 2 minutes, until the mixture is very fluffy and shiny and forms firm peaks. Turn off the mixer and check the peaks again. At this point, the slope should be nearly vertical.

* Divide the icing among the small bowls—the number depends on how many different colors of icing you want. Color each bowl of icing a different color by stirring in a few drops of food coloring. You can even make you own "custom" colors by combining food colorings. Cover each bowl with a damp, wrung-out paper towel and top with a piece of plastic wrap until you are ready to decorate, or a hard skin will form on top.

decorate the cookies

* Using the small offset spatula, spread the icing over the cookies, wiping the spatula clean each time you switch to a different colored icing. You can also pipe icing: Spoon some icing into a small disposable piping bag, cut a tiny hole in the bottom, and squeeze the bag gently to create patterns and shapes on your cookies. Or fill another icing tool, such as a squeeze bottle, and frost the cookies. While the icing is wet, add sprinkles or other decorations as desired. Let the icing dry for 1 to 2 hours. It will harden. Once it is hard, you can stack the cookies in an airtight container and store them at room temperature for up to 3 weeks.

PIES, TARTS, AND FRUIT DESSERTS

Fruit desserts are colorful, juicy,
sweet, and tart. Each fruit tells
you what season it is.

—BELLA

EASY PIE DOUGH

ingredients

½ cup (1 stick) cold unsalted butter
(keep refrigerated until needed)

5 tablespoons water

1¼ cups unbleached all-purpose
flour

2 teaspoons sugar

¼ teaspoon salt

tools

Measuring cups and spoons

1 small and 1 large bowl

Whisk

Pastry blender

Table knife

Table fork

Plastic wrap

Bench scraper

Parchment paper

Rolling pin

Small icing or offset spatula

Ruler

Pastry brush

Baking sheet

cut up the butter

✳ Cut the cold butter into small
cubes and refrigerate for 10 minutes. Put the water in a small bowl
and refrigerate at the same time.

> **Bella's tip:** The trick here
> is to keep the butter cold. Keep
> it in the fridge until you need it.
> Once the butter is in small pieces
> in the dough, if they start to feel
> warm and squishy, stop and refrig-
> erate the dough for 15 minutes,
> then continue with the recipe.

cut the butter into the flour

✳ Put the flour, sugar, and salt into
the large bowl and whisk until
blended. Scatter the cold butter
pieces over the dry ingredients
and toss them with your fingers
until they are coated with the flour.
Using the pastry blender, cut the
butter into smaller and smaller
pieces (see page 16). If any
chunks of cold butter get stuck
in the wires of the pastry blender,
use the table knife to push them
off, then continue cutting. You
are done when the mixture looks
like bread crumbs, with very tiny
pieces of butter in the flour.

mix the dough

✳ Sprinkle 4 tablespoons of the cold
water over the top of the flour-
butter mixture, then stir with the
fork about 25 times. The mixture will begin to hold together in
shaggy clumps (see left photo).
Grab a handful of the clumps and
some of the dry stuff at the bottom
and squeeze firmly. Open your
hand. The dough is ready when it
holds together, even if a few small
pieces fall off.

✳ If the clump falls apart and looks
dry, you need a little more water.
Before adding more water, remove
any large, moist clumps from the
bowl, and set them on your work
surface. Then add the remaining
tablespoon of cold water to the dry
crumbs in the bowl and stir again.

shape the dough

✳ Turn the clumps of dough out onto
the work surface. Gently knead it
all together 3 to 6 times, just until
blended into a smooth dough.
Press the dough into an 8-inch
circle, wrap in plastic wrap, and
refrigerate for 30 minutes. Use the
bench scraper to clean the work
surface.

roll out the dough

✳ Line the baking sheet with the parchment paper (see page 4). Dust the table generously with flour. Unwrap the chilled dough and place it in the center of the flour. Sprinkle a little more flour over the top.

Bella's tip: **Don't worry about putting plenty of flour on the table when you roll out the dough. As long as the dough is cool to the touch, it won't absorb the flour. If the dough starts to get warm and squishy, transfer it onto a baking sheet and refrigerate for 15 minutes, then continue rolling. The extra flour keeps the dough from sticking to the table, and you brush it all off at the end anyway.**

✳ Starting from the edge closest to you, roll gently but firmly to the edge opposite you and then back again twice. If the dough cracks when you try to roll it, it's too cold. Let it sit on the table for 8 to 10 minutes, then try to roll it again. Be careful not to roll the pin off the edge of the dough, or the dough will stick to the surface.

✳ Pretend the circle is a clock face, with 12 o'clock at the top. Turn the dough 2 hours, to 2 o'clock, and then roll up and back again twice. When you turn the dough, it should move easily. If it doesn't, gently lift the stuck area, loosening it with a small icing spatula, and sprinkle some more flour

underneath. Turn the dough 2 more hours and roll up and back again twice (see right photo). Repeat the rolling up and back and turning until the dough is a circle 14 inches across.

chill the dough

✳ Brush any flour from the top of the dough. Gently fold the circle into quarters, brushing off any excess flour as you fold. Transfer the folded dough to the prepared baking sheet. Unfold the circle so it is flat. Refrigerate while you prepare the filling for the pie.

3 5

TOP-CRUST JUMBLEBERRY PIE

ingredients

1 recipe Easy Pie Dough (page 46), prepared through step 6

filling

3 cups (12 ounces) fresh blackberries

1½ cups (6 ounces) fresh raspberries

1 cup (6 ounces) fresh blueberries

¾ cup sugar

3 tablespoons cornstarch

glaze

1 large egg

1½ teaspoons sugar

tools

Measuring cups and spoons

3 by 3-inch cookie cutter, in any shape (approximate size is okay)

Baking sheet

1 large and 1 small bowl

Silicone spatula or wooden spoon

9-inch pie dish

Small offset spatula

Small bowl

Table fork

Pastry brush

Parchment paper

Oven mitts

Cooling rack

1 cut the dough shapes

* Remove the chilled rolled-out dough from the refrigerator, and leaving the dough on the baking sheet, use the cookie cutter to cut out shapes from the dough. Cut the shapes as close together as possible so you won't have to reroll the dough scraps to cut out more. Put the baking sheet back into the refrigerator for 30 minutes, or in the freezer for 15 minutes.

2 prepare the oven

* Position an oven rack in the center of the oven, and preheat the oven to 400°F.

3 make the filling

* Turn each container of berries, one at a time, onto the baking sheet. Pick out and throw away any moldy or squished berries or anything that isn't fruit. You might find stems or leaves. Transfer the good berries to the large bowl. Continue until all the berries have been picked over and added to the bowl. Sprinkle the sugar and cornstarch over the berries and stir gently with the silicone spatula until all the berries are evenly coated. Scrape the filling into the pie dish.

4 top with the pie dough

* Remove the pie dough from the refrigerator and gently pop or peel off the dough shapes. The small offset spatula is helpful here. Arrange the dough shapes in slightly overlapping circles over the berries. Make the first circle around the edge of the pie dish and work toward the center. The filling should be almost completely covered. Depending on the shape of your cutter, there may be some holes here and there, and that's fine.

Pick different cookie-cutter shapes depending on the occasion. Try stars for the Fourth of July, or hearts for Valentine's Day.

—B

glaze the pie dough

✳ Crack the egg into the small bowl, and beat with the fork just until well blended. Brush a thin coating of egg over the dough (you won't use all the egg). Sprinkle the sugar evenly over the top of the pie. Line the baking sheet with parchment paper and place the pie on top.

bake the pie

✳ Bake for 40 to 45 minutes, until the pastry is golden brown and the berry juices are bubbling and thick. Using the oven mitts, transfer the baking sheet to the cooling rack and let cool for at least 10 to 15 minutes before serving. Serve warm or at room temperature.

playing around

You can make this pie with any kind of fruit. Just make sure you have about 6 cups berries or sliced fruit. The berries here are tart and juicy, but if you choose a fruit that is sweet, like strawberries or peaches, you can reduce the sugar to ½ cup and the cornstarch to 2 tablespoons.

You don't even need a pie pan for this recipe. It looks a little like a flying saucer filled with apples instead of aliens.

—B

RUSTIC APPLE PIE

before you begin

* Position an oven rack in the bottom 1/3 of the oven, and pre-heat the oven to 400°F.

make the filling

* Peel and core the apples (see page 13). Cut the apples into 1/4-inch-thick slices. Transfer the slices to the large bowl. Sprinkle the sugar, cinnamon, and corn-starch over the apples. Using the wooden spoon, gently stir the fruit until it is evenly coated with the sugar mixture.

assemble the pie

* Remove the rolled-out pie dough on the baking sheet from the refrigerator. Spoon the apple filling onto the circle, creating an even layer in the center and leaving a 2-inch-wide border uncovered around the edge of the dough. Fold the border up and over the filling, gathering the dough into pleats so it fits snugly around the fruit (see photo on next page). The center of the pie will be open.

ingredients

1 recipe Easy Pie Dough (page 46), prepared through step 6

filling

4 large (about 1¾ pounds total) Granny Smith apples

¼ cup sugar

¼ teaspoon ground cinnamon

2 teaspoons cornstarch

to finish

1 tablespoon unsalted butter, melted (see page 10)

2 teaspoons sugar

tools

Measuring cups and spoons

Vegetable peeler

Cutting board

Paring knife

Large bowl

Wooden spoon

Pastry brush

Metal spatula

Oven mitts

Cooling rack

3

playing around

You can substitute other fruit for the apples. Try peaches, plums, cherries, or berries. If the fruit is very tart, like sour cherries or tart plums, you may want to increase the sugar to about ½ cup. If it is really juicy, increase the cornstarch to 1½ tablespoons.

finish and bake the pie

✳ Brush the pleated dough edges with the melted butter, then sprinkle them with the sugar.

✳ Bake for 40 to 50 minutes, until the crust is a deep golden brown and the fruit is juicy and bubbling. Use the metal spatula to lift the pie slightly so you can look underneath. The bottom of the crust should be golden brown. Using the oven mitts, transfer the pan to a cooling rack and let the pie cool for 10 to 15 minutes before serving. Serve warm with a big scoop of ice cream.

NUTS FOR NUTELLA CHOCOLATE TART

ingredients

crust

1½ cups finely ground chocolate cookie crumbs (not sandwich cookies)

6 tablespoons (¾ stick) unsalted butter, melted (see page 10)

filling

4 ounces semisweet chocolate

⅔ cup heavy whipping cream

¾ cup Nutella (chocolate-hazelnut spread)

to decorate

1 tablespoon unsweetened cocoa powder

tools

Measuring cups and spoons

2 medium bowls

14 by 4-inch rectangular tart pan with removable bottom

Baking sheet

Silicone spatula

Oven mitts

Cooling rack

Cutting board

Serrated knife

Small saucepan

Whisk

Parchment paper

Rectangular stencil, in any design, about length of tart pan

Fine-mesh sieve

before you begin

* Position an oven rack in the center of the oven, and preheat the oven to 350°F.

make the crust

* Place the cookie crumbs in 1 of the medium bowls. Pour the melted butter over the crumbs and stir with the spatula until all the crumbs are evenly moistened. Smash any lumps that form.

* Scrape the mixture into the tart pan and use your clean fingers or the bottom of a measuring cup to press the mixture into a thin, even layer over the bottom of the pan. The excess will mound along the sides. Use your fingers to press this excess up the sides of the pan so that the crust is level with the rim. Set the tart pan on the baking sheet.

bake the crust

* Bake for 8 to 10 minutes, until it is fragrant. It will harden as it cools. Using the oven mitts, transfer to the cooling rack and let cool completely.

make the filling

* Put the chocolate on the cutting board. Using the serrated knife, chop the chocolate into small pieces (see page 11). Place the chocolate in the other medium bowl. Pour the cream into the small saucepan, place over medium heat, and heat just until it begins to simmer. Turn off the heat. Immediately pour the cream over the chocolate. Let sit for 2 minutes, then whisk gently until blended and smooth. Whisk in the Nutella until smooth (see left photo).

* Scrape the filling into the cooled tart shell with the clean silicone spatula and smooth the top. Refrigerate for about 1 hour, or until firm.

unmold the tart

* Carefully push the bottom of the tart pan up through the sides. Leave the tart on the bottom of the pan. Set on a piece of parchment paper.

decorate the top

* Place the stencil on top of the tart. It should be sturdy and have a pattern you like that covers the length of the tart. Place the cocoa powder in the sieve and hold it over the tart. Tap the side of the sieve gently as you slowly move it around the top of the tart (see right photo). Be careful not to tap too hard: You want a fine layer of cocoa, not thick piles that will make your guests cough! Carefully lift the stencil straight up from the tart, then slowly move it to the side, so you don't spill any more cocoa powder onto the tart.

This luscious tart is full of rich chocolate and hazelnut flavors. It looks so cool, your friends won't believe you made it yourself!

—B

A swirl of blueberry jam in the center of each biscuit makes this dessert as beautiful as it is deeeelicious.

—B

BLUEBERRY SWIRL COBBLER

①

before you begin

✱ Position an oven rack in the center of the oven, and preheat the oven to 375°F. Line the baking sheet with the parchment paper (see page 4).

②

make the filling

✱ Put the sugar in the large bowl. Using the rasp grater, grate the zest from the lemon over the bowl (see page 12). Using your fingers, mix the zest into the sugar. Then, mix in the cornstarch. Then, cut the lemon in half and juice it with the juicer (see page 12). Measure 2½ tablespoons juice and set aside to use later.

✱ Turn the berries onto the baking sheet. Pick out and throw away any moldy or squished berries, or stems or leaves. Put the berries in the colander and rinse under cool running water. Pat them dry with paper towels, and add them to the bowl with the sugar. Add the lemon juice and stir gently with the spoon until all the berries are evenly coated. Scrape the mixture into the baking dish and spread in an even layer. Set aside.

③

roll out the scone dough

✱ Sprinkle your work surface with a little flour. Set the dough on the flour, and sprinkle another tablespoon or so over the top. Shape the dough into a rough rectangle. Starting from the edge closest to you, roll gently but firmly to the edge opposite you and then back again twice. Be careful not to roll the pin off the edge of the dough, or the dough will stick to the surface. Turn the dough a quarter turn and roll up and back again twice. When you turn the dough, it should move easily. If it doesn't, gently lift the stuck area, loosening it with the small spatula, and sprinkle some more flour underneath. Repeat the rolling and turning of the dough until you have a 12 by 9-inch rectangle.

ingredients

fruit filling

¾ cup sugar

1 lemon

1½ tablespoons cornstarch

8 cups (about 2½ pounds) fresh blueberries

scone topping

1 recipe Crunchy-Top Vanilla Scones (page 62), prepared through step 3

⅓ cup blueberry jam

1 teaspoon sugar

Vanilla ice cream, for serving

tools

Measuring cups and spoons

Baking sheet

Parchment paper

Large bowl

Rasp grater

Citrus squeezer

Colander

Wooden spoon or silicone spatula

12 by 9-inch ceramic baking dish

Rolling pin

Small offset spatula

Ruler

Pastry brush

Bench scraper

Serrated knife

Oven mitts

Cooling rack

4

shape the blueberry rolls

* Brush any excess flour from the top of the dough. Use the bench scraper to clean any extra flour from the work surface around the dough. Gently fold the dough over and brush all the flour from the bottom of the dough. Position the rectangle so you are facing a long side.

* Using the small spatula, spread the jam in an even layer over the entire top of the dough except for a 1-inch-wide uncovered border along the long side opposite you.

* Starting at the long side closest to you, roll up the dough into a log, keeping it fairly tight as you go (see photo). When you reach the opposite side, roll the dough right on top of the uncovered border. Roll the log backward, so the seam is on top, and pinch all along it to seal it.

5

cut the rolls

* Using the serrated knife, cut the log crosswise into 4 equal pieces. Use a gentle sawing motion when you cut so that you don't flatten the log. Cut each quarter into 3 equal pieces, for a total of 12 rolls. Arrange the rolls on top of the blueberry filling in 3 rows of 4 rolls each, and sprinkle with the sugar. Refrigerate for 15 minutes.

6

bake the cobbler

* Set the baking dish on the prepared baking sheet. Bake for 40 to 45 minutes, until the fruit is bubbling and the biscuits are a nice golden brown. Using oven mitts, transfer to the cooling rack and let cool for 15 to 20 minutes before serving. Serve warm with a scoop of ice cream.

4

playing around

You can substitute 4½ pounds peaches, nectarines, apricots, or plums for the blueberries. Core and slice the fruit into ¼-inch slices, just like you would apples (see page 13). Add ¼ teaspoon spice, such as ground cinnamon or nutmeg, if you like. Pick a flavor of jam that you think goes well with your fruit. It doesn't have to match. For example, seedless raspberry jam is good with peaches. Look in the jams and jellies aisle at the supermarket for inspiration.

JOHNNY APPLE-SEED CRUMBLE

serves
6 to 8
apple lovers

before you begin

* Position an oven rack in the center of the oven, and preheat the oven to 350°F. Line the baking sheet with the parchment paper (see page 4).

make the filling

* Peel and core the apples (see page 13). Cut the apples into ¼-inch-thick slices. Transfer the slices to the large bowl. Sprinkle with the lemon juice and toss with the wooden spoon to coat evenly. Sprinkle with the brown sugar, cornstarch, and cinnamon and stir gently until the fruit is evenly coated. Scrape the filling into the pie dish. Set aside.

make the topping

* Cut the cold butter into small cubes and refrigerate for 10 minutes. Put the flour, sugar, and salt in the medium bowl and whisk until blended. Scatter the cold butter pieces over the dry ingredients and toss them with your fingers until coated with the flour. Using the pastry blender, cut the butter into smaller and smaller pieces (see page 16). If any chunks of cold butter get stuck in the wires of the pastry blender, use the table knife to push them off, then continue cutting.

* At first the mixture will look dry, but eventually it will begin to look like damp sand. At this point, put the pastry blender aside and rub the mixture gently between your fingers, pinching it until it forms small clumps the size of peas. Scatter the topping evenly over the apple filling, covering it completely.

bake the crumble

* Set the pie pan on the prepared baking sheet. Bake for 50 to 60 minutes, until the topping is nicely browned and the fruit is bubbling and soft. Test the fruit by sliding a paring knife into the center of the pan. It should slide in and out of the cooked fruit easily. Using the oven mitts, transfer the pan to the cooling rack and let cool for 15 to 20 minutes before serving. Spoon into bowls and serve with a big scoop of ice cream.

ingredients

filling

2½ pounds Granny Smith apples

2 teaspoons freshly squeezed lemon juice (see page 12)

½ cup tightly packed light brown sugar

1 tablespoon cornstarch

¾ teaspoon ground cinnamon

topping

½ cup (1 stick) cold unsalted butter

1 cup unbleached all-purpose flour

¾ cup sugar

¼ teaspoon salt

Vanilla ice cream, for serving

tools

Measuring cups and spoons

Baking sheet

Parchment paper

Vegetable peeler

Paring knife

Cutting board

1 large and 1 medium bowl

Wooden spoon

Deep 9-inch pie dish

Whisk

Pastry blender

Table knife

Oven mitts

Cooling rack

QUICK BREADS

You can make quick breads fast when you're hungry. They're also really easy, so you hardly need any help.

—BELLA

ingredients

scones

½ cup (1 stick) cold unsalted butter

¾ cup milk

1 tablespoon pure vanilla extract

2 cups unbleached all-purpose flour

¼ cup sugar

2½ teaspoons baking powder

¼ teaspoon salt

topping

1 tablespoon milk

3 tablespoons turbinado sugar

¼ teaspoon ground cinnamon

tools

Measuring cups and spoons

Baking sheet

Parchment paper

1 large and 2 small bowls

Whisk

Pastry blender

Table knife and fork

Ruler

Chef's knife

Pastry brush

Table spoon

Oven mitts

Cooling rack

Offset spatula (optional)

CRUNCHY-TOP VANILLA SCONES

1

cut up the butter and prepare the pan

* Cut the cold butter into small cubes and refrigerate for 10 minutes. Measure the milk, add the vanilla to it, and refrigerate it next to the butter.

* Line the baking sheet with the parchment paper (see page 4).

2

cut the butter into the flour

* Put the flour, sugar, baking powder, and salt in the large bowl and whisk until blended. Scatter the cold butter pieces over the dry ingredients and toss them with your hands until they are coated with the flour mixture. Using the pastry blender, cut the butter into smaller and smaller pieces (see page 16). If chunks of cold butter get stuck in the wires of the pastry blender, use the table knife to push them off, then continue cutting. You are done when the biggest butter pieces are no larger than green peas. Some will be much smaller, and that's fine.

These radically good scones with big vanilla flavor and crunchy sugar topping are great for breakfast, and perfect for strawberry shortcakes or blueberry swirl cobbler!

—B

3

mix the dough

✳ Pour the chilled vanilla milk into the butter-flour mixture, then stir with the fork 12 to 15 times, until it holds together in big, shaggy clumps. Sprinkle your work surface with a little flour. Turn the clumpy mass out onto the flour and knead it gently 4 to 8 times (see page 18), until it comes together into a dough. Don't knead too long—like you do for bread or pizza dough—or the scones will be tough.

4

shape and cut the dough

✳ Pat the dough into an 8 by 4-inch rectangle. Be sure it is the same thickness everywhere. Using the chef's knife, cut the rectangle in half the long way (lengthwise), and then into quarters the short way (crosswise). You should have 8 scones, each about 2 inches square. Brush off any extra flour from the top and bottom of the scones and place them several inches apart on the prepared baking sheet. Refrigerate for 20 minutes.

✳ Just after you slip the scones into the refrigerator, position an oven rack in the center of the oven, and preheat the oven to 425°F.

5

top and bake the scones

✳ To top the scones, pour the milk into 1 of the small bowls. Put the turbinado sugar and cinnamon in the other small bowl and stir together with the spoon. Brush the top of each scone with a thin coating of the milk. Sprinkle the cinnamon sugar evenly over the biscuits.

✳ Bake for 14 to 16 minutes, until golden brown on top and firm to the touch. Using the oven mitts, transfer the pan to the cooling rack. Let the scones cool for 5 minutes before serving. Transfer to serving plates with an offset spatula.

playing around

cheese biscuits

If you leave out the sugar and vanilla and add some grated cheese, you can turn vanilla scones into yummy cheese biscuits. Increase the salt to ½ teaspoon. At the end of step 2, just before you add the milk in step 3, stir ⅔ cup grated (see page 13) sharp Cheddar cheese, or whatever kind you like, into the dry ingredients. After you brush the tops with milk, leave off the cinnamon sugar and instead sprinkle the tops with an extra ⅓ cup grated cheese. The biscuits will take an extra minute or two longer to bake.

Strawberries are great in spring and summer when they are very red and sweet. But you can also make these shortcakes with raspberries, blackberries, peaches, or any fruit you like.

—B

SCRUMPTIOUS STRAWBERRY SHORTCAKE

ingredients

1 recipe Crunchy-Top Vanilla Scones (page 62)

strawberries

6 cups (2¼ pounds) fresh, ripe strawberries

3 tablespoons sugar

whipped cream

1½ cups heavy whipping cream

2 tablespoons sugar

1 teaspoon pure vanilla extract

tools

Measuring cups and spoons

Sieve or colander

Strawberry huller or 1-inch star piping tip

Paring knife

Cutting board

2 medium bowls

2 table spoons

Electric mixer or whisk

Table knife

mix and bake the scones

✳ Mix and bake the scones as directed and let them cool completely. You can make them a few hours ahead, if you like.

prepare the strawberries

✳ Place the berries in a sieve or colander, look through them, and discard any moldy berries. Rinse the remaining berries under cool running water. Drain well and pat dry with paper towels. Using the huller, star piping tip, or paring knife, remove the leafy green tops (hulls) from the strawberries (see page 12).

✳ Then, using the paring knife and the cutting board, cut the strawberries into ¼-inch-thick slices. Put the berries in 1 of the medium bowls, sprinkle with the sugar, and toss with a table spoon. Set aside and stir every few minutes. As the berries sit, the sugar will draw out some of their juices and make a tasty syrup in the bottom of the bowl.

whip the cream

✳ Put the cream, sugar, and vanilla in the other medium bowl. Using the mixer or whisk, whip the cream until it holds medium-firm peaks when the whisk or beaters are lifted (see page 17). It should look silky.

✳ If you whip the cream too long and it looks grainy, lumpy, or curdled, pour in 3 to 4 more tablespoons cream and stir in gently (no more whipping!). It should smooth out nicely. Cover and refrigerate until needed.

assemble the shortcakes

✳ Using the table knife, cut each scone in half. Put 1 of the "bottoms," cut side up, on each plate. Spoon the strawberries and syrup over the bottoms, dividing evenly. Place a large spoonful of whipped cream on top of each mound of strawberries. Set the biscuit tops, cut side down, on the cream. Serve right away.

ingredients

streusel topping

4 tablespoons tightly packed
light brown sugar

2 tablespoons unbleached all-
purpose flour

½ teaspoon ground cinnamon

2 tablespoons canola or corn oil

4 tablespoons chopped pecans
(or nut of your choice)

muffins

1½ cups unbleached all-purpose
flour

½ cup tightly packed light
brown sugar

½ teaspoon baking soda

1 teaspoon ground cinnamon

⅛ teaspoon salt

½ cup buttermilk

¾ cup canola or corn oil

1 large egg

2 teaspoons pure vanilla extract

tools

Measuring cups and spoons

12-cup standard muffin pan

Paper liners

1 small, 1 medium, and 1 large bowl

Table spoon

Whisk

Spring-loaded ice-cream scoop
(optional): 1 tablespoon

Toothpick

Oven mitts

Cooling rack

CINNAMON STREUSEL COFFEECAKE MUFFINS

before you begin

* Position an oven rack in the center of the oven, and preheat the
oven to 375°F. Line the muffin
pan with paper liners.

make the streusel topping

* Put the brown sugar, flour, and
cinnamon in a small bowl and stir
with the spoon to mix. Add the
oil and stir, smashing any large
lumps, until the mixture is an
even brown and looks like damp
sand. Stir in the nuts. Set aside.

make the muffin batter

* Put the flour, brown sugar, baking soda, cinnamon, and salt in
the large bowl and whisk to blend
well. Put the buttermilk, oil, egg,
and vanilla in the medium bowl.
Whisk to blend evenly.

* Make a well in the center of the
dry ingredients. Pour the liquid
ingredients into the well (see page
14). Whisk gently at first, and
then more vigorously until you
have a smooth batter. A few small
lumps are okay.

Bella's tip: **I like to use a
1-tablespoon-size ice-cream scoop
to fill the cups—it keeps things
neat and easy. I put one scoop in
the bottom, then streusel, then
2 more scoops on top, then more
streusel. It goes fast with the scoop.**

66

If you measure out everything the night before, it takes less than 5 minutes to mix and scoop the batter in the morning. Sometimes I like to sprinkle a few blueberries on top of each muffin before I add the streusel.

—B

fill the cups and bake

* Put a tablespoon of batter in each cup. Top with a generous teaspoon of the streusel topping. Divide the remaining batter evenly among the cups, about 2 additional tablespoons in each cup. The batter will fill the cups a little over halfway. Sprinkle a generous teaspoon of the streusel mixture over the top of each muffin.

* Bake for 17 to 20 minutes, until a toothpick inserted into the center of a muffin comes out clean. Using oven mitts, transfer the pan to the cooling rack.

playing around

silly feet

It's fun to bake these in the cartoon-like baking cups shown in the photo on page 67. You'll need 12 Silly Feet Baking Cups, evenly spaced on a baking sheet. Use the same size ice cream scoop (or 3 tablespoons of batter) to fill each baking cup. The batter will fill the cups about ¾ full. Bake for the same amount of time as described above. Be careful to keep the pan level when you are transferring it in and out of the oven—if you tilt the pan too much, the cups will fall over, as if you tripped them!

adding icing

These are also delicious with a little icing on top. In a medium bowl, use a spoon to stir together ½ cup powdered sugar and 2 teaspoons water until smooth. If it's too thick to drip off the spoon, stir in 1 more teaspoon of water.

Just after you transfer the muffin pan to the cooling rack, use a measuring spoon to drizzle about ½ teaspoon of the glaze over the top of each hot muffin. It will look a little melty and uneven. That's fine. Serve warm or at room temperature.

GONE BANANAS CHOCOLATE CHIP CAKE

serves
8
apes
(er, friends)

ingredients

banana cake

3 large, very ripe bananas

2 cups unbleached all-purpose flour

¾ teaspoon baking soda

½ teaspoon salt

2 large eggs

1 cup sugar

½ cup canola or corn oil

1 teaspoon pure vanilla extract

½ cup miniature semisweet chocolate chips

chocolate icing

4 ounces semisweet chocolate

½ cup heavy whipping cream

tools

Measuring cups and spoons

9 by 5-inch loaf pan

2 medium and 1 large bowl

Fork or potato masher

Whisk

Silicone spatula

Toothpick

Oven mitts

Cooling rack

Cutting board

Serrated knife

Small saucepan

Table spoon

1 *before you begin*

* Position an oven rack in the center of the oven, and preheat the oven to 350°F. Lightly butter the loaf pan, or spray with pan spray.

2 *mash the bananas*

* Peel the bananas and break them into pieces in 1 of the medium bowls. Using the fork or potato masher, smash them into pulp. It's okay if a few small lumps of banana remain. You should have about 1½ cups banana pulp.

mix the batter

✳ Put the flour, baking soda, and salt in the large bowl and whisk to blend well. Add the eggs, sugar, oil, and vanilla to the banana pulp and whisk to blend well. Make a well in the center of the dry ingredients and pour the banana mixture into the well. Whisk until the batter is smooth and you don't see any more patches of flour. Gently stir in the chocolate chips.

fill the pan and bake the cake

✳ Using the silicone spatula, scrape the batter into the prepared pan and smooth the top. Bake for 65 to 75 minutes, until deep golden brown, firm to the touch in the center, and a toothpick inserted into the center comes out clean (see page 7). You may see some melted chocolate on the toothpick from the chocolate chips. Using the oven mitts, transfer the pan to the cooling rack and let the cake cool completely.

make the icing

✳ When the cake is cool, make the icing. Put the chocolate on the cutting board. Using the serrated knife, chop the chocolate into small pieces (see page 11). Transfer the chocolate to the other medium bowl. Pour the cream into the small saucepan and place over medium heat, just until it begins to boil. Turn off the heat. Immediately pour the cream over the chocolate. Let the mixture sit for 2 minutes, then whisk gently until blended and smooth. Let cool for 5 to 10 minutes, until the icing runs off the tip of a teaspoon like warm honey.

ice the cake

✳ Remove the cake from the pan by turning it upside down and firmly shaking the pan a couple of times, while guiding the cake out onto your hand. Turn the cake right side up on a serving plate or a piece of parchment paper. Using the tablespoon, spoon the icing evenly over the top, letting some of it drip down the sides. Let the icing set for 20 minutes, then slice the cake with a serrated knife. Or leave the cake, uncovered, at room temperature until serving time.

This one is super-easy because you stir everything together in one big bowl. If you love chocolate-covered bananas, this is your cake.

—B

These airy puffs are crispy on the outside and soft on the inside. The centers are hollow, and they are the perfect little hiding place for a treat like jam or whipped cream.

—B

POPOVER BALLOONS

makes

12

puffy popovers

ingredients

1¼ cups milk

3 large eggs

2 tablespoons unsalted butter, melted (see page 10)

1 cup unbleached all-purpose flour

½ teaspoon salt

tools

Measuring cups and spoons

12-cup standard muffin pan

Blender

Oven mitts

Cooling rack

Small offset spatula

before you begin

❋ Position an oven rack in the center of the oven, and preheat the oven to 425°F. Generously butter the muffin pan, or coat with pan spray.

make the batter

❋ Put the milk, eggs, and butter in the blender. Put the lid on securely and blend on high speed for 1 minute. Turn off the blender, uncover, and add the flour and salt. Re-cover and blend on high speed for another minute.

fill the cups and bake the popovers

❋ Divide the batter evenly among the prepared muffin cups. It should come about ⅔ of the way up the sides of each cup.

❋ Bake for 30 minutes, or until deep golden brown and crispy. Using the oven mitts, transfer the pan to the cooling rack and let cool for 5 minutes before serving. Use the small offset spatula to run around the edges of each popover, to loosen them from the pan. Then pop each one out with the spatula and serve hot.

ingredients

1 cup unbleached all-purpose flour

1 cup fine cornmeal

¼ cup sugar

1½ teaspoons baking powder

1 teaspoon salt

1 cup milk or heavy whipping cream

2 large eggs

½ cup (1 stick) unsalted butter, melted (see page 10)

⅔ cup fresh or frozen corn kernels

tools

Measuring cups and spoons

24-cup mini muffin pan

Paper liners (optional)

Medium bowl

Whisk

2-cup liquid measuring cup

Table fork

Silicone spatula

Spring-loaded ice-cream scoop (optional): 2 tablespoon

Toothpick

Oven mitts

Cooling rack

MINI CORN BREAD MUFFINS

before you begin

✳ Position an oven rack in the center of the oven, and preheat the oven to 350°F. Lightly butter the muffin pan, spray with pan spray, or line with paper liners.

mix the batter

✳ Put the flour, cornmeal, sugar, baking powder, and salt in the medium bowl and whisk to blend well. Pour the milk into the 2-cup measuring cup. Crack the eggs into the milk, then stir with the fork until the eggs are fully blended with the milk.

✳ Pour the milk mixture and melted butter into the dry ingredients. Whisk gently at first, and then, as the mixture blends, whisk faster, until the batter is smooth and no dry patches are visible. Use the silicone spatula to stir in the corn kernels.

Bella's tips **Fresh sweet summer corn makes these even better. Ask an adult for help when cutting the kernels off a fresh ear of corn.**

③

fill the cups and bake the muffins

✳ Divide the batter evenly among the prepared muffin cups. The ice-cream scoop helps to do this quickly and neatly; otherwise measure 2 tablespoons of batter into each cup.

✳ Bake for 16 to 18 minutes, until the tops are firm to the touch and a toothpick inserted into the center comes out clean (see page 7). Using the oven mitts, transfer to the cooling rack and let the muffins cool for 5 minutes. Serve warm.

playing around

mini corn bread loaves

Butter or spray eight 4 by 2¼-inch mini loaf pans. Prepare the muffin mixture as directed in the recipe, then divide it evenly among the loaf pans, filling them about ½ full. Bake for 25 to 30 minutes, or until a toothpick inserted into the center comes out clean. Transfer to a cooling rack and let cool for 5 minutes. Serve warm.

standard-size corn bread muffins

Line a standard-size muffin tin with paper liners. Prepare the muffin mixture as directed in the recipe, then divide it evenly among the paper liners, filling them about ⅔ full. Bake for 20 to 22 minutes, or until lightly golden

and a toothpick inserted into the center comes out clean. Transfer to a cooling rack and let cool for 5 minutes. Serve warm.

bacon-cheddar corn bread muffins

Cook, cool, and break into small pieces 5 strips of bacon. Grate about ½ cup sharp Cheddar cheese and add it, with the bacon, after you have stirred in the milk and egg mixture. Divide the batter among 12 standard-size muffin cups lined with paper liners. Grate ⅓ cup additional Cheddar cheese and sprinkle a little over the top of each one. Bake for 22 to 26 minutes, or until lightly golden.

PB&J MUFFINS

1 · before you begin

* Position an oven rack in the center of the oven, and preheat the oven to 375°F. Line the muffin pan with paper liners.

2 · mix the batter

* Place the flour and baking powder in the medium bowl and whisk to blend. Set aside.

* Place the butter, brown sugar, and milk in the saucepan, and heat over medium heat until the butter is melted and the mixture is hot and steamy. Whisk a couple of times to make sure the mixture heats evenly. Turn off the heat. Add the peanut butter and vanilla to the saucepan and whisk until everything is blended and looks smooth. Add the egg and whisk to blend well.

* Use the silicone spatula to scrape the peanut butter mixture into the bowl with the flour. Stir gently at first, and then more vigorously until you have a smooth batter.

3 · fill the cups and bake the muffins

* Fill the bottom of each cup with one scoop of batter, filling them about ⅓ full. Spoon a tablespoon of your favorite jam or jelly on top. Top with another scoop of batter to fill the cups ¾ full.

* Bake for 17 to 20 minutes, or until the tops are golden brown and a toothpick inserted into the center of a muffin comes out clean; you'll see some jam on the toothpick, but there shouldn't be any raw batter. Using the oven mitts, transfer the pan to the cooling rack. Let cool for 10 minutes before serving.

ingredients

1½ cups unbleached all-purpose flour

1½ teaspoons baking powder

4 tablespoons (½ stick) unsalted butter, cut into pieces

⅔ cup tightly packed light brown sugar

⅔ cup milk

½ cup creamy peanut butter (or chunky), at room temperature

1½ teaspoons pure vanilla extract

1 large egg, at room temperature

¾ cup your favorite jam or jelly

tools

Measuring cups and spoons

12-cup standard muffin pan

Paper liners

Medium bowl

Whisk

Medium saucepan

Silicone spatula

Spring-loaded ice-cream scoop (optional): 1½ tablespoon

Toothpick

Oven mitts

Cooling rack

If you love PB&J sandwiches, you'll crave these for breakfast. They look like regular muffins, but each one has a hidden filling of jam in the center.

—B

CAKES

I like decorating cakes because I can swipe a taste of frosting when no one is looking.

—BELLA

This cake is fun because it doesn't have frosting on the sides, so you get to see all the pretty layers.

—B

CHOCOLATE CELEBRATION CAKE

makes
1
big yummy cake

ingredients

cake

1 cup water

¾ cup buttermilk

¾ cup canola or corn oil

3 large eggs

2 cups unbleached all-purpose flour

1¾ cups sugar

¾ cup unsweetened natural cocoa powder

2 teaspoons baking soda

¼ teaspoon salt

frosting

12 ounces cream cheese, at room temperature

6 tablespoons (¾ stick) unsalted butter, at room temperature

3 cups powdered sugar

2 teaspoons pure vanilla extract

tools

Measuring cups and spoons

2 (9-inch) cake pans

Parchment paper

2 medium and 2 large bowls

Whisk

Fine-mesh sieve

Silicone spatula

Toothpick

Oven mitts

2 cooling racks

Electric mixer

Small offset spatula

10- to 12-inch flat serving plate or cake stand

9-inch cake cardboard or tart pan bottom

---

before you begin

* Position 1 oven rack in the top ⅓ of the oven and 1 oven rack in the bottom ⅓ of the oven, and preheat the oven to 350°F. Lightly butter the cake pans or spray with pan spray. Line the pans with the parchment paper (see page 4).

2 make the cake batter

* Put the water, buttermilk, oil, and eggs in 1 medium bowl. Whisk until the eggs have completely blended into the mixture.

* Sift together the flour, sugar, cocoa powder, baking soda, and salt into 1 of the large bowls (see page 11). Push through any lumps with your fingers.

* Pour the liquid ingredients into the dry ingredients. Whisk gently at first, and then, as the mixture blends, whisk faster until you have a smooth batter and you don't see any more dry patches.

fill the pans and bake the cake layers

* Using the silicone spatula, scrape the batter into the prepared pans, dividing it as evenly as you can. Put 1 pan in the center of each oven rack. Bake for 30 to 35 minutes, until a toothpick inserted into the center comes out clean (see page 7).

* Using the oven mitts, transfer to the cooling racks. If the cakes are rounded on top, place a clean, dry kitchen towel on top of each hot cake and press down firmly with the palm of your hand to level the surface. Let cool completely.

Bella's tip: **There is lots of cool stuff you can use to decorate the cake. Look for colorful candles, sprinkles, confetti candy, or chunky sugar in the baking aisle. Check the candy aisle too for more ideas.**

make the frosting

❋ Place the room-temperature cream cheese and butter in the other large bowl. Using the mixer, beat on medium-low speed for about 2 minutes, or until creamy and smooth. Turn off the mixer. Sift half of the powdered sugar over the top of the cream cheese mixture. Turn on the mixer to medium-low speed and beat until thoroughly mixed. Turn off the mixer again, and scrape down the sides of the bowl with the silicone spatula. Sift in the remaining sugar and beat again until the mixture is blended and fluffy. Beat in the vanilla extract.

unmold 1 cake layer

❋ Slide the small spatula around the edges of the cake layers to loosen them from the pan. Place the serving plate upside down on top of 1 cake pan. Hold the plate and pan together like a sandwich, then flip them over. The cake will fall out of the pan onto the plate. Lift off the pan and peel off the parchment paper.

6

6

playing around

chocolate cupcakes

This cake batter makes great cupcakes. It makes 24 cupcakes, so you'll need to line 2 (12-cup) standard muffin pans with paper liners. Divide the batter evenly among the cups, filling them no more than ⅔ full. Bake on 2 racks as described for the cake layers for 15 to 20 minutes, until a toothpick inserted into the center of a cupcake comes out clean (see page 7). Let them cool completely on cooling racks before frosting them. If you like chocolate frosting, double the frosting on page 84 to frost 24 cupcakes.

6

frost and decorate the cake

✳ Using the offset spatula, scoop out about half of the frosting into a mound on the center of the cake. Then, spread the frosting evenly on top, leaving a ¼-inch-wide border uncovered around the edge. When you put the second layer on top, it will squish the frosting out to the edge.

✳ Place a cake cardboard on top of the second cake layer, then flip them over together and lift off the pan. Peel off the parchment paper. Gently push the cake off the board and into place atop the frosted layer (see left photo).

✳ Scoop the remaining frosting onto the top layer and spread evenly to the edges (see above photo). Decorate the top with sprinkles or whatever you like. You can leave the cake at room temperature for a few hours. Otherwise, refrigerate the cake until serving time

VANILLA CUPCAKES WITH CHOCOLATE FROSTING

ingredients

frosting

6 ounces semisweet chocolate

¾ cup heavy whipping cream

cupcakes

1½ cups unbleached all-purpose flour

¾ teaspoon baking soda

¼ teaspoon salt

3 large eggs, at room temperature

1 tablespoon pure vanilla extract

¾ cup (1½ sticks) unsalted butter, softened (see page 10)

¾ cup sugar

½ cup buttermilk

to decorate

Sprinkles, confetti candy, coarse sugar, or any edible decorations

tools

Measuring cups and spoons

12-cup standard muffin pan

Paper liners or silicone baking cups

Cutting board

Serrated or chef's knife

2 medium, 1 small, and 1 large bowl

Small saucepan

Whisk

Plastic wrap

Fine-mesh sieve

Table fork

Electric mixer

Silicone spatula

Toothpick

Oven mitts

Cooling rack

Small offset spatula

before you begin

＊ Position an oven rack in the center of the oven, and preheat the oven to 350°F. Line the muffin pan with the paper liners.

make the frosting

＊ Put the chocolate on the cutting board. Using the serrated knife, chop the chocolate into small pieces (see page 11). Transfer the chocolate to 1 of the medium bowls. Pour the cream into the small saucepan and place over medium heat, just until it begins to boil. Turn off the heat.

＊ Immediately pour the cream over the chocolate. Let the mixture sit for 2 minutes, then whisk gently until blended and smooth. Set aside to cool, whisking gently every 15 to 20 minutes, until the mixture has the consistency of a creamy frosting. You can even do this the night before, cover it with plastic wrap, and leave it on the counter.

Decorating cakes is the best part (next to eating them!). There are lots of different sprinkles, candies, and stencils you can choose from to turn these cute mini cakes into a party for your mouth.

—B

make the cupcake batter

* Sift together the flour, baking soda, and salt into the other medium bowl (see page 11). Crack the eggs into the small bowl and add the vanilla. Using the fork, beat the eggs lightly, just until evenly mixed.

* Place the softened butter and sugar in the large bowl. Using the mixer, cream the butter and sugar for 6 to 7 minutes, until they are very light, almost white, in color (see page 15). Turn off the mixer. Scrape down the sides of the bowl with the silicone spatula.

* With the mixer running on medium speed, add the egg mixture slowly, about a tablespoon at a time. Let each addition blend

into the butter completely (it will only take about 5 seconds) before adding the next. Once you are finished, turn off the mixer and scrape down the sides of the bowl.

* Add half the flour mixture to the bowl. Turn the mixer on low speed, and beat just until the flour mixture is blended in, then add half of the buttermilk. Beat it in on low, just until blended, then repeat with the remaining flour and buttermilk. Mix only until you don't see any more dry patches. Turn off the mixer. Scrape down the bowl one last time, and make sure there aren't any dry bits or butter clumps hiding in the bottom of the bowl.

fill the cups and bake the cupcakes

* Divide the batter evenly among the prepared muffin cups. They should be no more than ½ full. Bake for 20 minutes, or until the tops of the cupcakes are firm to the touch and a toothpick inserted into the center comes out clean (see page 7). Using oven mitts, transfer the pan to the cooling rack and let the cupcakes cool completely (at least 40 minutes) before topping with frosting.

frost the cupcakes

* Lift the cupcakes out of the pan and put them on your work surface or a piece of parchment paper. Divide the frosting evenly among the cupcake tops. There is enough frosting for about 2 level tablespoons on each cupcake. Use the offset spatula to spread it close to the edges. Decorate the top with sprinkles or whatever you like. You can keep the cupcakes at room temperature for 2 days, and after that store any leftovers in the refrigerator.

CHOCOLATE-PEANUT BUTTER CUPCAKES

makes
24
crazy-good
cupcakes

bake the cupcakes

* Bake the chocolate cupcakes as directed and let cool completely.

make the frosting

* Place the softened butter in the large bowl. Sift half of the powdered sugar over the top of the butter (see page 11). Using the mixer, beat on medium-low speed to blend it in thoroughly. Turn off the mixer and scrape down the sides of the bowl with the silicone spatula. Sift in the remaining powdered sugar and beat on medium-high speed for about 2 minutes, or until the mixture is blended and fluffy. Turn off the mixer and scrape down the sides of the bowl.

* Add the peanut butter and beat on medium-high until blended and smooth. Scrape down the bowl one last time, and make sure there aren't any pockets of sugar or peanut butter hiding in the bottom of the bowl.

frost the cupcakes

* Divide the frosting evenly among the cupcake tops. There is enough frosting for about 2 level tablespoons on each cupcake. Using a small offset spatula, spread it all the way to the edges. These are delicious just like this. If you like, decorate the top with Reese's Pieces or anything you like.

* You can keep the cupcakes at room temperature for 2 days. After that, store any leftovers in the refrigerator. The frosting gets really hard in the fridge, so let the cupcakes sit at room temperature for at least 30 minutes before serving.

ingredients

1 recipe Chocolate Celebration Cake batter baked into cupcakes (see Playing Around, page 83)

frosting

1¼ cups (2½ sticks) unsalted butter, softened (see page 10)

1¾ cups powdered sugar

1¼ cups creamy peanut butter (not natural style), at room temperature

to decorate

Reese's Pieces, cut-up peanut butter cups, or chocolate sprinkles (optional)

tools

Measuring cups and spoons

Large bowl

Fine-mesh sieve

Electric mixer

Silicone spatula

Small offset spatula

These are so good, I've seen people close their eyes and purr after taking a bite!

—B

This cake always makes me think of snuggling in front of the fire on a cold night. It's easy to whip up when you get the craving because you just stir everything together by hand.

—B

PUMPKIN GINGERBREAD

before you begin

* Position an oven rack in the center of the oven, and preheat the oven to 350°F. Generously butter the Bundt pan or spray with pan spray, then dust with the bread crumbs (see page 4).

make the cake

* Sift together the flour, ginger, baking soda, cinnamon, allspice, nutmeg, cloves, and salt into the large bowl (see page 11). Push through any lumps with your fingers. Whisk to blend evenly.

* Put the egg, sugar, and pumpkin in the medium bowl and whisk until well mixed. Add the oil, molasses, and water and whisk until smooth and blended.

* Pour the liquid ingredients into the dry ingredients. Whisk gently at first, and then, as the mixture blends, whisk faster until you have a smooth batter and you don't see any more dry patches.

fill the pan and bake

* Using the silicone spatula, scrape the batter into the prepared pan, and smooth the top.

* Bake for 45 to 50 minutes, until the top feels firm and a toothpick inserted into the center comes out clean (see page 7). Using the oven mitts, transfer to the cooling rack and let cool in the pan for 20 minutes. You need to turn this cake out of the pan while it is warm (but not hot).

unmold and finish

* Place the serving plate upside down on top of the cake. Hold the plate and pan together like a sandwich, then flip them over. Be sure to ask an adult for help if this is too tricky. The cake will fall out of the pan onto the plate. Lift off the pan. Serve the cake warm or let cool completely.

* Just before serving, place the powdered sugar in the sieve and hold it over the cake. Tap the side of the sieve gently as you move it slowly over the top, showering it evenly with sugar.

ingredients

pan preparation

2 tablespoons butter, melted

⅓ cup unseasoned fine, dried bread crumbs

cake

2 cups unbleached all-purpose flour

1 tablespoon ground ginger

1 teaspoon baking soda

¾ teaspoon ground cinnamon

½ teaspoon ground allspice

½ teaspoon ground nutmeg

¼ teaspoon ground cloves

¼ teaspoon salt

1 large egg

⅔ cup sugar

1 cup canned pumpkin puree (not pumpkin pie filling)

½ cup canola or corn oil

½ cup unsulfured light molasses

½ cup water

to finish

2 tablespoons powdered sugar

tools

Measuring cups and spoons

10-inch Bundt pan

Sieve

1 large and 1 medium bowl

Whisk

Silicone spatula

Toothpick

Oven mitts

Cooling rack

10- to 12-inch flat serving plate or cake stand

SWIRLY MILK CHOCOLATE AND CARAMEL CHEESECAKE

ingredients

crust

1½ cups fine graham cracker crumbs

1 tablespoon sugar

6 tablespoons (¾ stick) unsalted butter, melted (see page 10)

cheesecake

9 ounces milk chocolate

1½ pounds (24 ounces) cream cheese, at room temperature

1 cup sugar

3 large eggs, at room temperature

2 teaspoons pure vanilla extract

⅓ cup store-bought caramel sauce

tools

Measuring cups and spoons

9-inch springform pan

Baking sheet

Parchment paper

1 medium, 1 large, and 1 small bowl

Small saucepan

Silicone spatula

Oven mitts

Cooling rack

Double boiler

Electric mixer

Small spoon

Small offset spatula

Toothpick or paring knife

Small, flexible icing spatula

Thin, sharp knife

This two-tone cheesecake is pretty, and everyone loves it. It's best to make it the day before you want to eat it so that it has lots of time to chill.

—B

1

before you begin

* Position an oven rack in the center of the oven, and preheat the oven to 325°F. Lightly butter the springform pan or spray with pan spray. Line a baking sheet with parchment paper (see page 4).

2

make and bake the crust

* Place the graham cracker crumbs and sugar in the medium bowl. Pour the melted butter over the crumbs and stir with the silicone spatula until the mixture is evenly moistened. Smash any lumps that form.

* Scrape the mixture into the prepared pan and use your clean fingers or the bottom of a measuring cup to press the mixture into a thin, even layer over the bottom of the pan. The excess will mound along the sides. Use your fingers to press this excess 1 inch up the sides of the pan—it won't reach the top and will seem low, but it's fine.

* Set the springform pan on the prepared baking sheet. Bake for 10 minutes. Using the oven mitts, transfer to the cooling rack and let cool for 15 minutes. Leave the oven on.

make the cheesecake batter

* Using the double boiler, melt the milk chocolate (see page 12). When the chocolate is melted and smooth, leave it over the warm water while you make the cheese-cake batter.

* Put the cream cheese and sugar in the large bowl. Using the mixer, beat on low speed for 1 minute, or until blended. Turn off the mixer. Using the silicone spatula, scrape down the sides of the bowl and along the bottom. Beat on low speed for 1 minute more, or until the mixture is very smooth and free of lumps.

* Add the eggs, one at a time, beating after each egg is added for 10 to 15 seconds, until blended. Beat in the vanilla. Turn off the mixer, and scrape down the bowl again.

flavor the batter

* Remove ½ cup of the batter and scrape it into the small bowl. Add the caramel sauce to the small bowl and blend well with the small spoon. Set aside.

* Scrape the melted chocolate into the batter remaining in the large bowl. Blend on low speed for 30 seconds. Turn off the mixer, and scrape down the sides of the bowl. Beat on low speed for another 15 seconds, or until the mixture is evenly colored.

layer the batter in the pan

* Pour ½ of the chocolate batter into the graham cracker crust. Using the offset spatula, spread the batter in an even layer. Be careful not to scrape up the crust. Spoon about ¾ of the caramel mixture on top and spread it in an even layer. Top with the remaining chocolate batter and smooth the top.

swirl the caramel on top

* Using the small spoon, drizzle the remaining caramel batter over the top in thin lines. Drag the tip of the toothpick (or the tip of the paring knife) through the surface in a figure eight several times, until the lines are swirled and you like the way the design looks (see photo). Don't push the tip in too deep or you will scrape up bits of crust into the batter.

bake and cool the cheesecake

❋ Bake for 1 hour, or until the edges are set and puffed but the center still looks a bit wiggly when you tap the side of the pan with a table knife. Using the oven mitts, transfer to the cooling rack.

❋ Immediately run the flexible spatula around the inside edge of the pan to loosen the cake. You'll probably want to ask an adult for help with this part. If you don't loosen the sides of the cake from the pan, the cake will crack as it cools. Be sure to press the spatula against the pan sides so that you don't cut into the cake. Let the cake cool for at least 1½ hours, or until completely cooled. Then refrigerate for at least 4 hours before serving. Overnight is even better.

Bella's tip: **Always hold 2-piece pans—springform pans, tart pans with removable bottoms—by their sides. If you put your hands underneath, you could pop out the bottom by accident.**

unmold the cheesecake

❋ Run the spatula around the inside edge of the pan again, then unclip the clasp and lift the ring up and off the cake. Leave the cake on the pan bottom. Have a warm, damp kitchen towel handy. Cut the cake with a thin, sharp knife, carefully wiping the knife with the towel after cutting each slice. An adult might be helpful with this step, too.

playing around

You can substitute dark chocolate sauce for the caramel sauce and make a dark chocolate swirl. Or you can leave the swirl batter plain, for a pretty white swirl on top.

YEAST BREADS

I love kneading and stretching
the bread dough into any shape I want.
—BELLA

makes
1
delicious
loaf

ingredients

1¼ cups warm milk (no hotter than 120°F)

1 tablespoon active-dry yeast, or 2¼ teaspoons quick-rise yeast

2 teaspoons sugar

3¼ cups unbleached all-purpose flour

1½ teaspoons salt

4 tablespoons unsalted butter, melted (see page 10)

egg glaze

1 large egg yolk

1 teaspoon water

tools

Measuring cups and spoons

2 small and 1 large bowl

Small whisk or spoon

Wooden spoon

Bench scraper

Plastic wrap

9 by 5-inch loaf pan

Ruler

Pastry brush

Oven mitts

Instant-read thermometer

Cooling rack

1

proof the yeast

✳ Put ¼ cup of the warm milk in a small bowl. Add the yeast and sugar and whisk or stir to dissolve. Set the bowl aside for 8 to 10 minutes, until the mixture looks foamy (see page 11). If the yeast isn't foamy after 15 minutes, start over with a new package.

2

mix the dough

✳ Put the flour and salt in the large bowl and whisk to blend. Make a well in the center of the flour mixture, and pour the yeast mixture into the well. Then pour the remaining 1 cup warm milk and the melted butter into the well. Using the wooden spoon, stir together the flour mixture and the liquids until you get big, shaggy clumps of dough that start to stick together.

knead the dough

* Sprinkle a little flour on your work surface. You can always add more later, so don't sprinkle too much. Dump the dough clumps out of the bowl onto your work surface. Dip your hands in flour and start kneading the dough (see page 18). Keep kneading until the dough is smooth and springy and no longer sticky. It will take about 10 minutes. Lightly flour your hands and the surface if the dough starts sticking. It should feel tacky, like tape, but not sticky and gooey. The bench scraper is handy for scraping up any bits of dough stuck to the table, and to help you move the dough around.

let the dough rise

* Wash out the large bowl and rub the inside with a thin layer of vegetable oil or coat with pan spray. Shape the dough into a ball and put it in the bowl. Lightly rub or spray the top of the dough with a little oil. Cover the bowl with plastic wrap. Set the bowl aside and let the dough rise for 45 to 60 minutes, until it is twice as big.

punch down and shape the dough

* Butter the loaf pan or spray with pan spray. To punch down the dough, first clean your work surface, and lightly flour it again. Gently turn the dough out onto the surface. Press down firmly to flatten the dough and pop the air bubbles in it. Don't knead the dough, or it will get too springy to shape.

* To shape the dough into a sandwich loaf, gently pull the flattened dough into a 10 by 7-inch rectangle. Position the rectangle so you are facing a long side. Starting from the long side closest to you, roll up the dough into a big log, keeping the roll fairly tight as you go. When you reach the opposite edge, roll the log backward, so the seam is on top, and pinch all along the seam to seal it.

* Place the dough, seam side down, in the prepared pan. If the dough log is too long for the pan, scrunch the ends together to compress the loaf and make it shorter. If it is too short, roll it back and forth on the work surface, pressing gently to stretch it a bit. Once the dough is in the pan, press on it firmly to level it and fill the pan evenly.

let the dough rise and prepare the oven

* Lightly oil or spray the top of the dough to keep it moist. Cover the pan loosely with plastic wrap. Set the pan aside and let the dough rise for 45 to 60 minutes, until it is ½ inch above the rim of the pan.

* After the dough has risen for about 30 minutes, position an oven rack in the center of the oven, and preheat the oven to 400°F. That way, the oven will be ready when you are ready to bake.

glaze the dough

* Once the dough has risen, remove the plastic wrap and prepare the egg glaze. In a small bowl, whisk together the yolk and water thoroughly. Using the pastry brush, brush the top of the dough with a thin coating of the glaze. You won't need all of it.

8

bake and cool the bread

✳ Bake the bread for 35 to 40 minutes, until it is a rich golden brown. If you're not sure if it is ready, take its temperature with an instant-read kitchen thermometer. Using the oven mitts, remove the loaf from the oven and close the oven door. Set the pan on the stove top. Stick the thermometer in the side of the loaf, just above the rim of the pan, so the end of the thermometer is in the center of the loaf. It should read 200°F. If you need to bake the bread longer, be sure to pull out the thermometer before the bread goes back in the oven.

✳ Using the oven mitts, remove the pan from the oven and place it on the cooling rack. Let it cool for 20 minutes, then carefully pull the loaf out of the pan and set it on the rack. Let cool completely before slicing.

pretzels

Position 1 oven rack in the top ⅓ of the oven and 1 oven rack in the bottom ⅓ of the oven, and preheat the oven to 425°F. Line 2 baking sheets with parchment paper (see page 4).

When you get to step 5 in the bread recipe, punch down the dough, then use a bench scraper to cut the dough into 12 equal pieces. Place 1 piece of the dough on a clean, dry work surface. Using your palms, roll the piece into a rope 20 inches long. To shape the pretzel, first form the rope into a U. Then fold over the right end of the U and press it onto the left side of the bottom of the U. Repeat with the left end of the U, pressing it onto the right side (see page 96). Repeat with the remaining dough pieces.

Evenly space 6 pretzels on each prepared pan. Brush the pretzels with a thin coating of the egg glaze, then sprinkle them with a little coarse salt. Set the pans aside and let the dough rise for 10 minutes.

Bake for 7 minutes. Using the oven mitts, switch the pans between the oven racks. Bake for another 6 to 7 minutes, until golden brown. While the pretzels are baking, melt 4 tablespoons unsalted butter (see page 10). When the pretzels are ready, transfer the baking sheets to cooling racks and brush with the melted butter.

monkey bread

Prepare a 9 by 5-inch loaf pan as directed in the bread recipe.

To make the butter and sugar coating, melt ½ cup (1 stick) unsalted butter (see page 10). Don't let it boil. Pour the melted butter into a medium bowl.

In another medium bowl, stir together 1¼ cups sugar and 4 teaspoons ground cinnamon until well mixed.

When you get to step 5 in the bread recipe, use a bench scraper or scissors to cut the dough into 35 to 40 pieces the size of big, fat cherries. Toss 5 or 6 dough pieces in the melted butter, coating evenly. Use your fingers to lift out the pieces—pause a moment over the bowl so the excess butter drips back into it—and drop them into the cinnamon sugar. Toss them to coat evenly. Then transfer them into the prepared loaf pan. Coat the remaining pieces the same way. When all of the dough pieces are in the pan, gently press them so there are no air pockets, they fill the pan evenly, and the top is level.

Cover the pan loosely with plastic wrap. Set the pan aside and let the dough rise for 45 to 60 minutes, until it is about ½ inch above the rim of the pan. After 30 minutes, position an oven rack in the center of the oven, and preheat the oven to 375°F.

Set the loaf pan on a baking sheet, to catch any drips, and bake for 40 minutes, or until deep golden brown. Transfer to a cooling rack and let cool for 20 minutes before eating. Ask an adult to help you lift the bread out of the pan while it's warm, then pull it apart with you fingers and enjoy!

I like the way some of the sugar melts into the bottom of the pan and gives the bottoms of the rolls a sweet, sticky glaze.

—B

SOFT AND SWEET CINNAMON ROLLS

1

make the filling

* While the bread dough finishes rising, put the brown sugar and cinnamon in the medium bowl and whisk together until well blended. Smash any brown sugar lumps to break them up. Set aside. Crack the egg into 1 of the small bowls and beat with the fork until blended. Set aside.

2

roll out the dough

* Sprinkle 3 tablespoons flour on the work surface. Turn the risen dough out of the bowl onto the floured surface and shape it into a rough rectangle. Sprinkle another tablespoon of flour on top. Starting from the edge closest to you, roll gently but firmly to the edge opposite you and then back again twice. Be careful not to roll the pin off the edge of the dough, or the dough will stick to the surface. Turn the dough a quarter turn and roll up and back again twice. When you turn the dough, it should move easily. If it doesn't, gently lift the area of stuck dough, loosening it with the small metal spatula, and sprinkle some more flour underneath. Repeat the rolling up and back and turning of the dough until you have a 15 by 12-inch rectangle.

ingredients

1 recipe of The Amazing Shape-Changing Bread (page 96), prepared through step 4

filling

1½ cups tightly packed light brown sugar

1½ tablespoons ground cinnamon

1 egg

icing

1 cup powdered sugar, or a little more if needed

1½ tablespoons water

tools

Measuring cups and spoons

1 medium and 2 small bowls

Whisk

Table fork

Rolling pin

Small offset spatula

Ruler

Large pastry brush

Bench scraper

Small pastry brush

10 by 2-inch cake pan

Serrated knife

Plastic wrap

Oven mitts

Cooling rack

Spoon

shape the rolls

✳ Brush any excess flour from the top and bottom of the dough with the large brush, and clean up any extra flour from around the dough with the bench scraper. Position the rectangle so you are facing a long side.

✳ Using the small pastry brush, brush a thin coating of egg all over the top of the dough. (You won't need all of it.) Use your fingers to scrape the filling onto the dough and spread it evenly over the surface, leaving a 1-inch-wide border uncovered along the long side opposite you.

✳ Starting at the long side closest to you, roll up the dough into a log, keeping it fairly tight as you go. When you reach the opposite side, roll the dough right on top of the uncovered border. Roll the log backward, so the seam is on top, and pinch all along the seam to seal it.

cut the rolls

✳ Lightly butter the cake pan or spray with pan spray. Using the serrated knife, cut the log crosswise into 10 rolls, each about 1½ inches wide. Use a gentle sawing motion when you cut so that you don't flatten the log. Arrange the rolls in the prepared cake pan, evenly spacing 8 rolls around the edge of the pan and putting 2 rolls in the center.

let the rolls rise and prepare the oven

✳ Cover the pan with plastic wrap and set in a warm place. Let the rolls rise for about 1 hour, or until they are nearly twice as big and fill almost all of the open spaces in the pan.

✳ After the rolls have risen for about 30 minutes, position an oven rack in the center of the oven, and preheat the oven to 350°F. That way, the oven will be ready when you are ready to bake.

bake the rolls

✳ Bake the rolls for 30 to 35 minutes, until they are golden and the sugar is bubbling around the edges. Using the oven mitts, transfer the pan to the cooling rack. Let cool for 10 to 15 minutes.

make the icing and ice the rolls

✳ Put 1 cup powdered sugar in the other small bowl. Add the water and whisk until well blended and completely smooth. The icing should be fairly thick, because it thins out when it hits the warm rolls. If it is thin and runny, add a little more sugar.

✳ Using the spoon, drizzle the icing over the tops of the warm rolls in any pattern you like. Eat them while they are warm!

CHEESE-Y PIZZA

1
proof the yeast

✳ Put ¼ cup of the warm water into the small bowl. Add the yeast and sugar and whisk or stir to dissolve. Set the bowl aside for 8 to 10 minutes, until it looks foamy (see page 11). If the yeast isn't foamy after 15 minutes, start over with a new package.

2
mix the dough

✳ Put the flour and salt in the large bowl and whisk to blend. Make a well in the center of the flour mixture, and pour the yeast mixture into the well. Then pour the remaining 1 cup warm water and the olive oil into the well. Using the wooden spoon, stir together the flour mixture and the liquids until you get big, shaggy clumps of dough that start to stick together.

3
knead the dough

✳ Sprinkle a little flour on your work surface. You can always add more later, so don't sprinkle too much. Dump the dough clumps out of the bowl onto your work surface. Dip your hands in flour and start kneading the dough (see page 18). Keep kneading until the dough is smooth and springy and no longer sticky. It will take about 10 minutes. Lightly flour your hands and the surface if the dough starts sticking. It should feel tacky, like tape, but not sticky and gooey. The bench scraper is handy for scraping up any bits of dough that are stuck to the table, and to help you move the dough around.

makes
2
12-inch
party pizzas

ingredients

pizza dough

1¼ cups warm water (no hotter than 120°F)

1¼ teaspoons active-dry yeast, or 1 teaspoon quick-rise yeast

¼ teaspoon sugar

3¼ cups unbleached all-purpose flour

1½ teaspoons salt

3 tablespoons olive oil

toppings

½ cup favorite tomato sauce

1½ cups (6 ounces) grated mozzarella cheese

20 to 30 slices pepperoni (optional)

Chopped cooked vegetables, like mushrooms, onions, or broccoli, or cooked meats of choice, such as crumbled sausage or sliced chicken (optional)

tools

Measuring cups and spoons

1 small and 1 large bowl

Small whisk or spoon

Wooden spoon

Bench scraper

Plastic wrap

2 baking sheets

Parchment paper

Rolling pin (optional)

Pastry brush

Ruler

Metal spoon

1 or 2 large offset metal spatulas

Oven mitts

2 cooling racks

Cutting board

Pizza wheel or chef's knife

4

let the dough rise and prepare the oven

✳ Wash out the large bowl and rub the inside with a thin coating of vegetable oil or mist with pan spray. Shape the dough into a ball and put it in the bowl. Lightly rub or spray the top of the dough with a little oil. Cover the bowl with plastic wrap. Set the bowl aside and let the dough rise for 45 to 60 minutes, until it is twice as big.

✳ After the dough has risen for about 30 minutes, prepare the oven. You can make 2 or 4 pizzas. To bake them all at one time, position 1 oven rack in the center of the oven and 1 rack in the bottom ⅓ of the oven, and preheat the oven to 475°F. To bake 1 pan at a time, position the oven rack in the bottom ⅓ of the oven.

✳ Line the baking sheets with the parchment paper (see page 4).

5

punch down and shape the dough

✳ To punch down the dough, first clean your work surface, and lightly flour it again. Turn the dough out of the bowl onto the floured surface. Press down firmly to flatten the dough and pop the air bubbles in it. Don't knead it, or it will get too springy to shape. Using the bench scraper, divide the dough into 2 equal pieces for making large pizzas, or into 4 pieces for making smaller pizzas.

✳ If making large pizzas, shape each piece of dough into a 12-inch circle. If making smaller pizzas, shape each piece of dough into an 8-inch circle. You can use a rolling pin to roll the dough into a circle (see page 19), or you can just press down and gently stretch the dough with your hands. You might need a little flour on your work surface to keep it from sticking. You can also lift the dough onto the back of your hands and stretch it by slowly pulling your hands apart (see photo). If you get a hole in the dough, just pinch it back together with your fingers. If the dough is too springy to shape, leave it on the work surface, cover it with plastic wrap, and let it rest for 15 minutes, then finish shaping it.

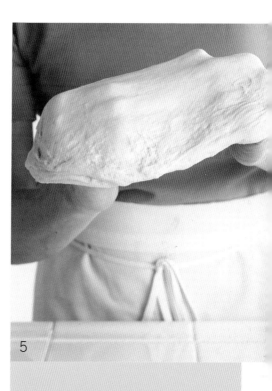

5

Bella's tip: **If you have a pizza stone and pizza peel, you can make pizza like a real chef. You have to heat the pizza stone in the oven for 40 minutes first, so that it's super-hot. That's what makes the crispy crust. And you'll need to sprinkle some semolina or flour on the pizza peel and assemble the pizzas one at a time on the peel. Make sure there is enough semolina that the pizza can slide around on the peel. Have an adult help you transfer it to the stone, and then take the pizza out when it's finished. Once you get the hang of it, you can do it yourself.**

top the pizzas

✳ When the circles are the shape and size you want, brush off any excess flour on the top and bottom. Put the pizzas on the prepared baking sheets.

✳ Using a metal spoon, spread ¼ cup of the tomato sauce on each large pizza, or 2 tablespoons on each smaller pizza, leaving a ½-inch-wide border uncovered all around the edge. Sprinkle the cheese evenly over the sauce. If you want, add pepperoni or another meat and a vegetable or two. Be creative, but keep in mind that 2 or 3 toppings are best. If you put on too many, your pizza will be soggy.

bake the pizzas

✳ You can put both baking sheets into the oven at the same time, 1 on each rack, or put the pans in one at a time on the lower rack. Bake the pizzas for 7 to 10 minutes, until the edges are golden brown. Using the metal spatula, lift the edge of the crust and look at the underside to make sure it is golden, too. If you are baking 2 pans at the same time, after 4 to 5 minutes, using the oven mitts, switch the pans between the racks. This will help the pizzas to bake more evenly. Also, when you have 2 pans in the oven, your crusts will take a few minutes longer to get brown and crispy.

✳ Using oven mitts, transfer the pans to the cooling racks. Using the large spatula—or 2 spatulas if you have made big pizzas—transfer the pizzas to a cutting board one at a time. You might need to ask an adult to help you with this step. Using the pizza wheel, cut the pizza into slices. Serve right away.

thinking ahead

Refrigerate the pizza dough overnight

Make the dough through step 4. Press out the air bubbles as described in the beginning of step 5, then divide the dough into 2 or 4 equal pieces, and shape each piece into a ball. Dust a baking sheet lightly with flour, put the balls on the pan, cover with plastic wrap, and refrigerate overnight. The next day, take the dough out of the refrigerator and set it on the counter for 15 to 20 minutes before shaping it into crusts as described in the second part of step 5.

Freeze the pizza dough for up to 6 weeks

Shape the dough into balls as described for refrigerating it overnight, then put each dough ball into a 1-quart-size resealable plastic freezer bag, squeeze out as much air as possible, and seal tightly. Place the bags in the freezer for up to 6 weeks. To thaw, transfer the bag of dough to the refrigerator the night before you want to bake the pizza. Or if you forget, just put the bag of frozen dough on the counter until it is thawed. Then proceed with shaping it into crusts as described in the second part of step 5.

GOTCHA FOCACCIA

proof the yeast

* Put ¼ cup of the warm water into the small bowl. Add the yeast and sugar and whisk or stir to dissolve. Set the bowl aside for 8 to 10 minutes, until it looks foamy (see page 11). If the yeast isn't foamy after 15 minutes, start over with a new package.

2

chop the rosemary

* While the yeast is proofing, chop the rosemary. Pick all the green leaves off the rosemary stem, and throw the stem away. Use the chef's knife and the cutting board to chop the rosemary leaves into very small pieces. Ask an adult for help, if you need it. Set aside.

3

mix the dough

* Put the flour and salt in the large bowl and whisk to blend. Make a well in the center of the flour mixture, and pour the yeast mixture into the well. Then pour the remaining 1 cup warm water and the olive oil into the well, and add the chopped rosemary, too. Using the wooden spoon, stir together all of the ingredients until they are evenly moist.

knead the dough

* Instead of kneading the dough on a work surface, stir it in the bowl with the spoon about 100 times. When your arm gets tired, switch hands. If you are making the dough with somebody else—a brother, a sister, a friend—take turns stirring. The dough will look springy and stretchy when you grab some with the spoon and try to lift it out of the bowl.

ingredients

dough

1¼ cups warm water (no hotter than 120°F)

2 teaspoons active-dry yeast, or 1½ teaspoons quick-rise yeast

½ teaspoon sugar

1 (6-inch) sprig rosemary

2½ cups unbleached all-purpose flour

1 teaspoon salt

3 tablespoons olive oil

for the top

2 tablespoons olive oil, plus a little extra

1 teaspoon coarse salt

tools

Measuring cups and spoons

1 small and 1 large bowl

Whisk or spoon

Chef's knife

Cutting board

Wooden spoon

Plastic wrap

Pastry brush

10 by 2-inch round cake pan

Oven mitts

Cooling rack

Serrated knife

5

let the dough rise

* Cover the bowl with plastic wrap. Set the bowl aside and let the dough rise for 45 to 60 minutes, until it is twice as big.

6

punch down and shape the dough

* Brush the pan generously with olive oil. Use the wooden spoon to stir the dough quickly about 15 times. You want to pop the big bubbles that formed when the dough was rising.

* Scrape the dough into the prepared cake pan. Brush the 2 tablespoons olive oil on top, then press and stretch the dough so it fills the bottom of the pan in an even layer.

7

let the dough rise and prepare the oven

* Cover the pan with plastic wrap. Set the pan aside and let the dough rise until it is nearly twice as big. This will take 45 to 60 minutes.

* After the dough has risen for about 30 minutes, position an oven rack in the center of the oven, and preheat the oven to 400°F.

8

dimple and bake the dough

* When the dough is done rising, take off the plastic wrap, rub a little olive oil on your fingers, and imitate "cat claws": Gently press the tips of your fingers into the dough, all the way down to the bottom of the pan, to create dimples. Do this with both hands 2 or 3 times only. You don't want to deflate the dough completely. Sprinkle the top of the dough evenly with the coarse salt.

* Bake the focaccia for 25 minutes, or until deep golden brown. Using the oven mitts, transfer the pan to a cooling rack. Let cool in the pan for 10 to 15 minutes before serving. Cut it into wedges with a serrated knife. You can either cut it in the pan, or remove it from the pan and cut it on a cutting board.

playing around

If you love olives, put them in your focaccia! Tear 10 pitted Kalamata olives in half and press them into the top of the dough after you dimple it.

CHOCOLATE CHUNK BREAD PUDDING

serves

8

warm friends on a cold night

ingredients

½ loaf bread, such as white bread, challah, or Italian bread

6 ounces semisweet chocolate

2 large eggs

2 large egg yolks

1 cup sugar

¼ teaspoon salt

1¾ cups milk

1¾ cups heavy whipping cream

2 teaspoons pure vanilla extract

Whipped cream and/or caramel sauce, for serving

tools

Measuring cups and spoons

9 by 2-inch ceramic pie dish or round cake pan

Serrated knife

Cutting board

Baking sheet

Cooling rack

Medium bowl

Whisk

Plastic wrap

Silicone spatula

Spoon

1

before you begin

* Position an oven rack in the center of the oven, and preheat the oven to 325°F. Lightly butter or spray the baking dish.

2

cut up the bread

* Place the bread on the cutting board. Using the serrated knife, cut the crust off the bread and throw the crust away. Then cut or tear the bread into ½-inch cubes or pieces. Be sure to ask an adult for help if this is too tricky. Spread the cubes on the baking sheet and bake for 20 minutes—this will dry out the bread so it can soak up the custard. Using oven mitts, transfer the baking sheet to the cooling rack and let cool completely.

* Measure out 4 cups of bread cubes and set aside for the pudding. Transfer any remaining bread cubes to a resealable plastic bag and store in the cupboard (or freezer) for another use.

3

chop the chocolate

* Put the chocolate on the cutting board. Using the serrated knife, chop the chocolate into small pieces (page 11). Set aside until needed.

4

make the custard

* In the medium bowl, whisk together the eggs, egg yolks, sugar, and salt until completely blended. Whisk in the milk, cream, and vanilla and blend well. Add the toasted bread cubes to the bowl and stir them into the custard. Cover with plastic wrap and refrigerate for 20 minutes, then remove the bowl from the refrigerator and stir the mixture, to make sure the bread soaks up the custard evenly. Return to the refrigerator for another 10 to 20 minutes, or until the bread has soaked up most of the custard and looks very soft.

5

bake the bread pudding

* Remove the plastic wrap and using the silicone spatula, stir the chopped chocolate into the mixture. Make sure the chocolate is evenly distributed. Scrape the mixture into the prepared baking dish and press it into an even layer. Bake the bread pudding for 50 to 70 minutes, or until slightly puffed, golden brown, and set in the center.

* To check, use the oven mitts to remove the dish from the oven. Set it on the stove and close the oven door. Use a spoon to press down firmly in the center of the bread pudding. The pudding is done when the center feels firm. If the custard pools around the spoon, return it to the oven and bake for another 10 to 15 minutes, then check again. Transfer to the cooling rack and let cool for 15 to 20 minutes before serving. Serve with whipped cream and/or caramel sauce. Cover any leftovers and refrigerate for up to 4 days. Reheat in a 325°F oven for 20 to 25 minutes, or until warmed through.

This recipe is a great way to use up almost any type of leftover bread. Sometimes I make bread just so I can have bread pudding!

—B

playing around

double chocolate bread pudding

Prepare the pan as directed in the original recipe. Melt 8 ounces of semisweet chocolate in a double boiler (see page 11). After you have blended the milk, cream, and vanilla into the custard, add the melted chocolate and immediately whisk well to blend the chocolate into the custard. Add the toasted bread, stir well, then cover with plastic wrap. Let the mixture sit in the refrigerator overnight—this will allow the dark custard to soak all the way to the center of each piece of bread. Once or twice during this time, remove the dish from the refrigerator and stir the mixture, to make sure the bread soaks up the custard evenly. Chop 5 ounces of milk chocolate (see page 11). Just before scraping the pudding into the baking dish, stir in the milk chocolate pieces. Bake as directed in the recipe.

chocolate cherry bread pudding

Prepare the pan as directed in the original recipe. Prepare the bread pudding as directed. After you stir the 5 ounces of chopped semisweet chocolate into the pudding, stir in 1 cup dried sour cherries. Bake as directed in the recipe.

Note: You can skip the cherries and add any dried fruit you like to this recipe, such as raisins, dried blueberries, dried cranberries, or larger dried fruit that you have snipped into small pieces with a pair of kitchen scissors, such as dried apricots, figs, or dates.

chocolate raspberry bread pudding

Prepare the pan as directed in the original recipe. Turn a half-pint container of fresh raspberries onto a baking sheet. Pick out and throw away any moldy or squished berries or anything that isn't fruit. You might find stems or leaves. Set aside the clean berries. Make the custard as directed. After you stir the 5 ounces of chopped semisweet chocolate into the pudding, gently stir in the raspberries. Bake as directed in the recipe.

cinnamon-scented bread pudding

Prepare the pan as directed in the original recipe. After you have whisked together the eggs, yolks, and sugar, add 1½ teaspoons ground cinnamon and blend well. Add the milk, cream, and vanilla, and continue as directed in the recipe. Leave out the chopped chocolate. Bake as directed in the recipe.

banana and chocolate bread pudding

Prepare the pan as directed in the original recipe. Use a fork to mash 2 large ripe and super soft bananas until they are soupy (a few lumps are okay). After you have blended the milk, cream, and vanilla into the custard, whisk in the smashed bananas. Add the toasted bread and continue with the recipe as directed. If you like, you can leave out the chocolate chunks, or switch to milk chocolate instead of semisweet chocolate. Bake as directed in the recipe.

Acknowledgments

When we were deciding what would be our next book, it was an easy decision to create a kids' baking book. Our kids' culinary camps consistently sell out and Cindy Mushet, who regularly bakes with her daughter, Bella, is the author of our award-winning book *The Art and Soul of Baking*. It was an unquestionable synergy we couldn't pass by.

And what a book this is. Bella and her mom give *Baking Kids Love* a wonderful, engaging tone. And the other kids in the book, who all have participated in our kids' camps in San Francisco, help make *Baking Kids Love* fun and colorful, and as Bella says, "deeeelicious." Thanks to Cindy for being our baking muse and to Bella for kid testing the recipes. Without the assistance of Barbara Dimas from our Maiden Lane store, who recruited Max Sherwood, Samantha Degnan, Isabella Vazirani, Blyth Galicia, and Blyth's sister Lyric Webb, we would have never had so much fun making the book both approachable and inviting for our youngest bakers.

Thanks also to our amazing photographer Maren Caruso and our designer Alison Lew, who captured the essence of our message. They were ably assisted by Maren's assistant, Stacy Ventura; prop stylist Kerrie Walsh and her assistant, Christine Wolheim; and food stylist Kim Kissling and her assistant, Sarah Fairhurst. Without the help of John Walker and his staff at the Maiden Lane store, David Bauer and Mark Beard at our distribution center, Kate Dering and Claudia Saber in our buying office, and the unflinching support of the folks at Andrews McMeel, especially Kirsty Melville, Jean Lucas, and Tammie Barker, all the pieces would not have been assembled into this joyful expression of our love for kids baking.

Here's to spending more time with our kids baking and to enjoying the sweetness life has to offer.

—SUR LA TABLE

Thanks to the amazing A-team of cookbook publishing: Sur La Table with guiding light Doralece Dullaghan; Andrews McMeel with visionary Kirsty Melville and superb editor Jean Lucas; and the gifted art and design squad of Alison Lew, Maren Caruso, Kim Kissling, Kerrie Walsh, and the whole crew who helped to make the book so much visual fun. Thanks to the kids—Max, Samantha, Isabella, and Blyth—who took time away from family and video games to join us in the photography studio. Special thanks to Kathi Saage, angel on my shoulder. And, of course, thanks to Bella, whose sweet presence is a constant inspiration, in and out of the kitchen.

—CINDY MUSHET

Index

09 10 11 12 13 SDB 10 9 8 7 6 5 4 3 2 1

LIBRARY OF CONGRESS CATALOGING-IN-PUBLICATION DATA

Mushet, Cindy, 1960-
  Baking kids love / Sur La Table with Cindy Mushet ; photography by Maren Caruso. — 1st ed.
     p. cm.
  Includes index.
  ISBN-13: 978-0-7407-8345-6
  ISBN-10: 0-7407-8345-9
  1. Baking-Juvenile literature. I. Sur La Table (Firm) II. Title.
  TX765.M885 2009
  641.8'15—dc22

                                  2009014414

COVER PHOTOGRAPHY: Maren Caruso
DESIGN: Vertigo Design NYC
FOOD STYLIST: Kim Kissling
ASSISTANT FOOD STYLIST: Sarah Fairhurst
PROP STYLIST: Kerrie Sherrell Walsh
ASSISTANT PROP STYLIST: Christine Wolheim
PHOTO ASSISTANT: Stacy Ventura

Baking Kids Love is a trademark belonging to Sur La Table, Inc., of Seattle.

www.andrewsmcmeel.com
www.surlatable.com

ATTENTION: SCHOOLS AND BUSINESSES
Andrews McMeel books are available at quantity discounts with bulk purchase for educational, business, or sales promotional use. For information, please write to: Special Sales Department, Andrews McMeel Publishing, LLC, 1130 Walnut Street, Kansas City, Missouri 64106.

CLOCKWISE: Samantha Degnan, Lyric Webb, Isabella Vazirani, Blyth Galicia, Max Sherwood, and Bella Robinson

About the authors

SUR LA TABLE AND CINDY MUSHET coauthored *The Art and Soul of Baking* (2008), which received the 2009 IACP Cookbook Award for Baking, was chosen by *Gourmet* magazine as a book club selection, and was a finalist for the 2009 baking book of the year by the James Beard Foundation. They continue to receive high praise for their contribution to the baking world.

SUR LA TABLE is the trusted authority when it comes to all things cooking related. Recognizing the importance of nurturing young chefs, Sur La Table offers gear and cooking classes made just for kids. Sur La Table entices aficionados and curious beginners alike with its amazing selection of cookware, bakeware, tools, cookbooks, and cooking school programs designed to make any cook's life easier. The original store and headquarters are in Seattle, Washington.

CINDY MUSHET has been a professional pastry chef and baking teacher for over twenty years. Her recipes have appeared in publications across the country, including *Bon Appétit, Fine Cooking, Country Home*, the *National Culinary Review*, and the *New York Times*. Inspired by her daughter, Bella, Cindy has taught baking to many children, both in school classrooms and in summer baking camps. A fun and engaging teacher, Cindy has also taught thousands of adults nationwide. She makes her home in the Los Angeles area.